NEW BIRKDALE

The Growth of a Lancashire Seaside Suburb
1850–1912

Birkdale Municipal Buildings.

NEW BIRKDALE

The Growth of a Lancashire Seaside Suburb
1850–1912

Harry Foster

First published in the U.K. in 1995 by
The Birkdale and Ainsdale Historical Research Society,
20, Blundell Drive, Birkdale, Southport, PR8 4RG

Produced for the Society by
Alan Sutton Publishing Ltd, Stroud, Glos.
Printed in Great Britain by
Hartnolls, Bodmin, Cornwall.

CONTENTS

BIRKDALE AND AINSDALE HISTORICAL RESEARCH SOCIETY

New Birkdale is the fourth in the Society's series of publications and shares the aims of its predecessors. We are attempting to find new material about the district and then to present it in a manner which will bring enjoyment and pleasure to readers. We are always grateful to have access to any historical material which relates to Birkdale and Ainsdale.

Sylvia Harrop,
Publication Editor

PREVIOUS PUBLICATIONS

Sylvia Harrop, *Old Birkdale and Ainsdale: Life on the south-west Lancashire Coast 1600–1851*, B & A Historical Research Society (1985)

Peggy Ormrod, *Birkdale and Ainsdale Past and Present: The 1845 tithe map superimposed on a modern street plan*, B & A Historical Research Society

Sylvia Harrop (ed.), *Families and Cottages of Old Birkdale and Ainsdale*, Carnegie Publishing (1992)

Further details from: Mrs. P.M. Perrins,
20 Blundell Drive,
Birkdale.

ILLUSTRATIONS

TABLES

PREFACE

This book is the sequel to Sylvia Harrop's *Old Birkdale and Ainsdale*, which told the fascinating and previously little-known story of this area's early years. *Old Birkdale* took the story to the coming of the railway in the mid-nineteenth century. In preparing this book, it became evident that little has been published about the later history of Birkdale, hence the present volume – *New Birkdale*.

The Victorians and Edwardians have left us a mass of evidence about their lives. A walk through Birkdale allows us to see many of their homes, churches, schools, parks, hotels, clubs and shops. On dusty shelves are to be found the minute books of Council committees, estate papers, school and church papers, whilst throughout our period local papers provided reports and commentaries on contemporary happenings. The census returns are a further rich source of information on all the residents. It is still possible to call on memories from old residents to gain insights into life in Birkdale in the early years of this century, while contemporary maps and photographs further enrich our understanding. This book attempts to unravel the story of how residents, landowners, politicians and entrepreneurs have shaped Birkdale since 1850, up to the point when it was amalgamated with Southport in 1912.

ACKNOWLEDGEMENTS

Many residents of Birkdale have contributed to my understanding of the township's history, particularly those who have attended local history talks, which I have given over many years. There is invariably someone in the audience who is able to contribute some further insight. I am also very grateful to have had the opportunity to work with the enthusiasts of the Birkdale and Ainsdale Historical Research Society, under the energetic leadership of Sylvia Harrop. The members include Reg Baxter, Terence Burgess, Audrey Coney, Joan Diggle, Bill Limont, Rene Merritt, Pat Perrins, Bill Pick and Peggy Ormrod. The contributions and mutual support available within the Society have lightened the task of collecting source material, and provided an important sounding board for the author. Although the book owes much to this collaboration, the interpretations are my own, and I must be held responsible.

Particular thanks for direct help with this volume are due to: Mr. K. Hall, former Lancashire County Archivist; Miss Janet Smith, formerly Liverpool City Archivist; Miss Margaret Proctor and Mr. Neil Sayer of the Merseyside Record Office; Mrs. Janet Jenkins, Miss Joan Tarbuck, and Mr. Roger Hull of Sefton Libraries; Miss Chris Ainsbury; Mr. Michael Braham; Mrs. D. Brown; Mrs. Ann Coates; Mrs. Sylvia Chapman; Messrs. Mark Chatterton, Geoffrey Dixon, Chris Driver; Dr. Eric Glasgow; Mr. Peter Gibb; Mrs. J. Leech; Messrs. Alan Marshall, Bryan Marshall, John Masters; Mrs. Brenda Pearson; Messrs. Ken Porter, Robin Rimmer and Geoff Wright.

Finally special thanks are due to: Sylvia Harrop, the Society's Publication Editor; Pat Perrins, the Society Secretary; Peggy Ormrod, who prepared the map of Old Birkdale; Alan R. Whittaker, who did the photographic work; the trustees of the Elsie Talbot Bridge Trust who provided a grant for computer and photographic work; Bill Marsden, who earlier helped to shape my approach to local history; and my wife Thelma, for tolerance, encouragement, and necessary criticism.

Harry Foster,
October 1994.

CHAPTER ONE

INTRODUCTION

A NEW BLUNDELL AND A NEW BIRKDALE

The said Trust Estates are particularly eligible for the Purposes of building, and it would be very beneficial to the said Thomas Weld-Blundell . . . if Power were given to grant Leases for terms not exceeding Ninety-nine Years of all or any Part of the Lands and Hereditaments . . . being Parts of the said Trust Estates which are situate in the aforesaid Parishes of Sefton, Walton on the Hill, and North Meols, and are adjacent to the Sea Shore in the same Parishes.
11 & 12 Victoria Cap 15, 31st August 1848

The Township of Birkdale, in the Parish of North Meols, had the sea for its western boundary, the Township of Southport to the north, the peaty plain of Halsall to the east, and the tall sandhills of Ainsdale to the south. In the 1840s it was an agricultural community, whose occupational and social make-up had not changed in any really significant way since the eighteenth century. The previously neglected history of how the inhabitants had wrested a living, from both land and sea, has already been told by Sylvia Harrop in *Old Birkdale and Ainsdale*. Of the Township's 2,100 acres, 545 acres were arable, 315 acres meadow and pasture, 40 acres taken up with the sites of buildings and gardens, whilst more than half the area, 1,200 acres, was sand-hills and rabbit-warrens. At the census of 1841 Birkdale contained only 556 inhabitants living in 99 houses, the population of the Township having increased by just over a half since 1801.

By contrast, in the adjoining part of North Meols, a similar rural economy had been transformed by the fashionable popularity of sea bathing. This led to vigorous growth, and the creation of the Township of Southport. It developed initially as a bathing resort and later as a place of residence. This settlement had sprung up close by the boundary with Birkdale, but as Birkdale was a separate manor, owned by a different landowner, expansion occurred in Southport only. The 1848 Ordnance Survey map dramatically demonstrates the contrast between the two townships, with the boundary between them being sharply defined where development ceased. On the last day of September, 1848, however, the following advertisement appeared in the *Southport Visiter*:

BIRKDALE – The proprietor of the Township of Birkdale has intimated his intention of granting long leases for building purposes on very liberal terms. The land adjoins to Southport, and has a frontage of three miles to the shore. We believe that the Township will be laid out under the superintendence of eminent surveyors and landscape gardeners, so that the plan will meet the views as well of those who would wish to possess marine residences of considerable extent as of those who would desire to erect single houses or shops. There is no doubt that this healthy locality will ultimately be covered with elegant and beautiful residences, suitable for the habitation of the most respectable parties.

These revolutionary proposals were the result of an equally dramatic change in the ownership of Birkdale. In the early seventeenth century, Birkdale was one of various manors purchased from Sir Cuthbert Halsall by Robert Blundell, of Ince Blundell, near Crosby. His great-great grandson, Henry Blundell was the most famous member of this family. It was he who spent large sums of money collecting both ancient sculptures and statuary, and pictures. Ince Blundell Hall was not large enough to hold his collection, so first he built a garden temple in the grounds for this purpose; and then, from 1802 onwards, a Pantheon. When he died in 1810 he left behind a house full of treasures.

Ince Blundell Hall in 1847.

2

Unfortunately, he also left behind family dissension and bitterness. He had fallen out with his only son, Charles, largely because of the latter's refusal to marry, and thus perpetuate the Blundell line. Relations between the two were so strained that Henry left the richest part of his estates (but not Birkdale) to his two married daughters. Charles contested this decision but lost. He died aged 76, in 1837, but was still to have his revenge. Embittered by the treatment he had received, he left the whole of his estate, not to a nephew, but to a very distant relative, Thomas Weld of Lulworth. There was, however, a discrepancy in Charles' will – presumably not deliberate – in that he had referred to Thomas Weld as Edward Weld. Nevertheless, this was sufficient to give his sisters hope that they might successfully challenge the will, and the family was once again contesting a law suit. This one dragged on for ten years, during which period

Coat of Arms of Thomas Weld-Blundell.

3

Ince Blundell Hall was uninhabited, and there was no undisputed Lord of the Manor of Birkdale. The sisters finally lost their case in the highest court of appeal, the House of Lords, on June 26th 1847. Thomas Weld gained possession of the Blundell lands, including Birkdale, and, in compliance with the terms of Charles Blundell's will, the new owner had taken by Royal Licence the name and arms of Blundell, in addition to his own, and become Thomas Weld-Blundell. The combined arms were surmounted by the crests of both families, the collared squirrel of the Blundells and the wyvern of the Welds. The Weld motto "Nil Sine Numine" (Nothing without God) was adopted.

The new Lord of the Manor had incurred considerable expense in the protracted series of court cases. In addition, the estate had been neglected for many years. Income from agricultural land could not compare with the ground rents received by urban landlords such as the Earls of Derby and Sefton in Liverpool, or Fleetwood-Hesketh and Scarisbrick in Southport, and it was to the possibility of urban development that Weld-Blundell turned his attention. The success of Southport, and the artificially abrupt termination of development at the Township boundary, pointed to the potential of Birkdale. There were, however, still some legal difficulties. Some of the land which he wished to develop was part of the Trust Estates involved in Charles Blundell's will, and the conditions of the trust had to be changed if he was to proceed with his plans. He therefore put a private Bill before Parliament giving him the power to grant leases of up to 99 years on land in Birkdale. The Act of Parliament was passed on August 31st 1848, and within a month he had placed his first advertisement. His solicitor's records show that he had anticipated the success of his Bill and had been working on plans for the urban development of Birkdale as early as 1846.[1]

NEW BIRKDALE: TWO SIDES OF THE RAILWAY TRACKS

It is no secret that Birkdale, practically, may be divided into two sections. That the line of demarcation, both topographically and pecuniary, is very sharp. On one side of the line are wealthy ratepayers and on the other ratepayers not wealthy.

Southport Visiter, 28th July 1871

Thomas Weld-Blundell adopted a property marketing strategy similar to that being introduced into neighbouring Southport by the Scarisbrick Estate. He sought to develop some of his land as a socially select area for prosperous middle-class residents. His advertising referred to 'beautiful villas', 'handsome', 'elegant and beautiful residences' for 'the most respectable parties'. This was no high-minded desire to create a model town, it was sound commercial sense. If he could lease his land in large plots, which were deep in relation to their frontage, the cost of providing streets was reduced. Also, by

4

offering relatively short 99 year leases, the building of high-class villas ensured a valuable reversionary interest. As Birkdale's single landowner, Weld-Blundell was in a position to exercise complete control over development. He offered leases of large plots, stipulating minimum values for the buildings, and protected the nature of the development through strict covenants. Having a wish to develop such an estate was not, however, sufficient to ensure that it happened. The editor of the *Southport Visiter* demonstrated that he understood the speculative nature of such ventures by his use of italics. He referred to: "The new town, with its pleasure grounds and gardens, and its superior dwelling houses and shops, which are *intended* to be erected on this uncultivated waste." Residents had to be attracted, and for this a number of conditions had to be met.

Residential suburbs have to be accessible, and Weld-Blundell demonstrated that he was well aware of the importance of railways. He appears to have anticipated the successful outcome of his court case and, for several years, had been active in promoting railway companies with lines servicing the estate. He had been nominated provisional chairman of the West Lancashire, or Liverpool, Southport and Preston Junction Railway as early as 1845. Although there had been massive local backing for a railway link for Southport, this company's proposed route, via Ormskirk, was very circuitous. Fortunately, the promoters withdrew in favour of other companies who were proposing direct lines. A Parliamentary Bill for the Liverpool, Crosby and Southport Railway Company received royal assent in June 1847. Weld-Blundell had earlier transferred his support to the new company. Both he and his neighbour William Blundell of Crosby Hall, the chairman of the Liverpool, Crosby and Southport Railway Company, gave their land, as did other landowners over whose land the projected railway was routed. The contemporary *J.S. Guide* suggests that these gifts were made ". . . in a spirit of highly creditable enterprise and patriotism." There was also a high degree of self-interest. Despite the severe economic depression, the project went ahead. The route, along the sandy coastal strip, provided no problems of gradient, or foundations, and only a single major bridge over the River Alt was required. Consequently, the line was completed within a three-month period and was opened on July 24th 1848, when the locomotive 'Sefton' pulled a carriage from Waterloo, the temporary southern terminus, to Southport. This modest local railway, contemptuously dubbed 'the shrimp line' by other railway companies, would enable Birkdale, along with other places on its northern line, to compete with the well-established southern suburbs of Liverpool, which were linked to the centre by tramway. The day after the opening the *Liverpool Mercury* reported:

> We hope ere long to see the land along the railway studded with beautiful villas, surrounded by modest foliage in which "the merchant princes". . . may spend their leisure hours in some ease and retirement.

Although it was not until October 1850 that the line into Sandhills was completed, thus giving direct access from Liverpool to Southport, Weld-Blundell had started his campaign to market 'Marine Villas' in Birkdale shortly after the opening in 1848. Not surprisingly, early advertisements emphasised that: "The Township is traversed by the Liverpool, Crosby and Southport Railway throughout its whole extent." The opening of a railway link with Liverpool and, via Southport, with inland Lancashire was to be a major factor in the development of Birkdale.

Within their suburbs, middle-class residents desired social exclusiveness, a condition which Weld-Blundell as the single landowner could ensure. The area he chose for a high-class residential estate was the sparsely populated Aindow Hills, west of the railway line, and immediately adjacent to the Southport boundary. The *Southport Visiter* described the area as an "uncultivated waste", hardly a fair reflection on the toil of the farmers who had eked out a meagre living from this agriculturally hostile environment. The scattered farms and cottages had to give way to the bricks and mortar of the villas. Physical boundaries, which helped to preserve social seclusion, were highly valued. In Birkdale the sea to the west and tall dunes in the south were perfect. Where natural boundaries did not exist developers sometimes created them, for example in south Liverpool seclusion was found behind tall sandstone walls. The railway provided a convenient inland barrier in Birkdale. The remaining margin, the boundary with Southport, was marked by a small water course, and Weld-Blundell initially allowed only one carriage way, that from Lord Street, to link the two townships.

During the early nineteenth century, the Victorians had "discovered" scenery and looked for fine views, open country and trees. Relatively flat, Birkdale could offer sea views only from its frontage, a feature emphasised in the advertisement. Tree growth was restricted to stunted willow scrub. The Victorians had, however, found an answer to such physically limited sites – residential parks, where landscape gardeners compensated for nature's shortcomings. In 1848, Prince Albert opened Prince's Park in Liverpool, which was quickly surrounded by high-class villas. Weld-Blundell's marketing recognised this factor – his suburb was to be known as Birkdale Park and the promotion emphasised the role to be played by ". . . eminent surveyors and landscape gardeners." In fact he had commissioned Edward Kemp, the superintendent of Birkenhead Park, to produce a scheme. In accord with the wording of the Weld-Blundell Estate Act, the plan shows an ambitious layout with a central circus, crescents and esplanades. Nevertheless Weld-Blundell was not prepared to spend vast sums on creating these amenities in an attempt to stimulate development. He did not wish to share the fate of Fleetwood-Hesketh, who had run into financial difficulties by doing just that at Fleetwood. It was the crippling demands of his ambitious plans for Fleetwood which

Lady Adelaide de Trafford visiting Aindow's Farm, Birkdale Park in 1862.

forced Peter Fleetwood-Hesketh to sell his Southport estates to his younger brother Charles, the Rector of North Meols.

An aspect in which Birkdale could score most heavily was the search for suburbs with a salubrious climate – the health factor. Smoke from industrial, and indeed from adjoining high-density domestic property, was to blight some suburban 'Park' developments in and around major towns. Birkdale Park was free from such nuisance and the prevailing winds brought clear fresh air (or ozone as Victorians preferred to call it) from over the Irish Sea. Weld-Blundell's advertisements described Birkdale as a "healthy locality", and it was marketed as a health resort.

The middle classes also looked for the proximity of cultural and social amenities, and a shopping centre. Urban development in neighbouring Southport had come to an abrupt end at the Birkdale boundary. Geographically Birkdale Park developed away from this boundary as a suburb of Southport, and its residents were able to share the latter's wealth of public and private facilities. In laying the foundation stone for St. James' Church, in Birkdale Park, in 1856, Charles Hesketh, the Rector of North Meols, described Birkdale as ". . . this extension of Southport, for I can call it no other, they are essentially one."

In the following year the *Southport Visiter* described Birkdale as ". . . this delightful suburb of Southport", whilst John Aughton, the builder of the first villa in Birkdale Park, predicted that "There is no doubt that at some time Southport and Birkdale will become one important town." The detailed account of how, after an uncertain start, Birkdale Park prospered as a high class residential suburb is told in Chapters Three and Four.

Although the wealth of Birkdale Park dominated the Township, there was another and very different area of New Birkdale inland of the railway. Here, alongside the Birkdale boundary, was the Ecclesfield district of Southport. This was a densely crowded working-class enclave. The landowners, the Scarisbrick Estate, provided no sanitation, no drainage, no piped water, no made surface for the roads, no pavements, and no piped gas.[2] Again Weld-Blundell followed the example of the Scarisbrick Estate and allowed this low-status district to spill over into Birkdale, into the Grove Street area. As the single landowner, Weld-Blundell could control where this cheap building was to be allowed. Later, further housing of this mean character was confined to the inland margin of Birkdale, in and around what is now Compton Road and Stamford Road. This area was well away from Birkdale Park, but not too remote to prevent labourers from walking to their employment. Between this uniformly low-status property and the railway was a mixed transitional zone of respectable working-class and lower middle-class dwellings. Beyond Liverpool Road, higher-status property was to appear, although not of the grandeur of Birkdale Park. The story of the socially complex area of New Birkdale inland of the railway is told in Chapter Five.

A detailed map produced by the Birkdale and Ainsdale Historical Research Society shows that the rural population of "Old Birkdale" had been scattered across the Township. Although there was no focal point of church or manor house, the greatest density was on the Common where there was something of a centre, well to the south of Birkdale Park. It was the site of the eighteenth century village school, which had lapsed early in the nineteenth century, a not uncommon occurrence at this time.

> There was no school nearer than Churchtown, and those who were ambitious of acquiring knowledge of the 3R's had to trudge five miles or so night and morning, to gratify their legitimate ambitions.[3]

The energy of Charles Hesketh, the new evangelical Rector of North Meols, led to the building of a new school on the old site in 1839. An undated manuscript contains the testimony of Alf Sawyer, aged 91 who recalled that:

> He ordered the tenants (farmers) to do the carting of brick and other materials to build a school for the poor people of the Common.[4]

BIRKDALE

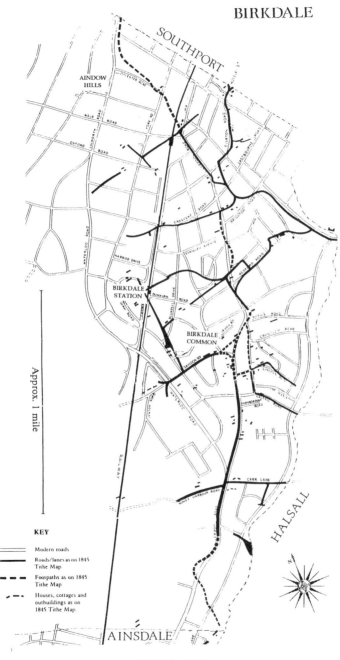

Birkdale, 1845.

The brick building consisted of one long room with a pine floor and no ceiling. As well as being a school, the room was used for religious services. It is interesting to note how the Rector had acted, during the absence of a Lord of the Manor, pending the outcome of the prolonged court case. The tithe apportionment of 1847 also showed two shops in the cottages of the Common.

The first Birkdale station was built in 1848 near the end of what is now Dunkirk Road, at the nearest point to the centre of the settlement at Birkdale Common. The Common also had an inn – the Ash Tree – a "little white country

Birkdale's first Railway Station.

10

public house", but this was some way from the school. Visits to the Ash Tree and the nearby 'Isle of Wight' were a popular excursion for visitors to Southport. It was said to be no uncommon thing to see 30 or 40 animals and a dozen or twenty donkey carriages tethered in front of the Ash Tree.

Birkdale Common was remote from the development of New Birkdale, and in 1851 the large majority of the male heads of household were farmers or agricultural workers. In Chapter Seven development on the Common is considered, with particular attention given to the role of agriculture, and the growing influence on the Common of the urban expansion in New Birkdale.

Most towns grow outwards from their centre, but, as New Birkdale was a suburb of Southport, it grew from the boundary. It was only late in the century that Birkdale developed a town centre of its own, around the railway station. The story of its emergence is told in Chapter Six.

Before considering the very varied development which took place in different parts of Birkdale, attention is given, in Chapter Two, to the landowners – Thomas Weld-Blundell and his son Charles – and to the Birkdale local authority. Chapter Eight is devoted to the bitter struggle which took place between the landowner and the local authority in order to determine the ownership of Birkdale beach.

CHAPTER TWO

NEW BIRKDALE: THE LANDOWNERS AND LOCAL AUTHORITY

Thomas Weld-Blundell

> . . . in coming into the estates great improvements were made by the new squire upon an extensive estate, which had been much neglected by his predecessor.
>
> *Southport Visiter*, 6th January 1887

Having secured the Lancashire estates, which had suffered from a long period of neglect, Thomas Weld-Blundell set about improving them. His promotion of Birkdale brought an urban dimension to what had been an agricultural estate, and his lands, with a value of £35,000, were soon producing an annual revenue of £20,000. Although the day-to-day dealings in Birkdale were efficiently discharged by his agent, Weld-Blundell paid close attention to the strategic decisions, mostly by correspondence, and proved to be a shrewd and prudent landowner.

Thomas Weld-Blundell was, however, a countryman at heart and had a more intimate knowledge of his rural estates than of suburban Birkdale. The Derby, Sefton, Scarisbrick and Weld-Blundell estates were the four great rural estates of south-west Lancashire. From Ince Blundell, he frequently visited farms, on foot or by carriage, and his ". . . personal interest in the working of his estate was proverbial in the district."[1] As a countryman, he was a keen sportsman. In south-west Lancashire this mainly meant shooting. The low-lying extensively-farmed land did not support a local hunt. Weld-Blundell was an excellent shot and remained so until a very late period of his life. Like most of the neighbouring landowners, he was an enthusiastic supporter of the local Waterloo Cup Meeting:

> On one occasion, however, a race between his greyhound, and a hound belonging to Lord Sefton resulted in a tie, but the judge giving his decision in favour of Lord Sefton's animal so annoyed Weld-Blundell that he ceased any further connection with coursing.[2]

Weld-Blundell restored Ince Blundell Hall, a large house of brick and stone built in the first half of the eighteenth century. The house stands in an attractive walled deer park. Nevertheless, like the other major local landowners, Weld-Blundell spent little time in Lancashire. It was only during the summer months that the family – he had eleven children – lived there. In 1858 he bought a small boat for his eldest son, Charles, to sail on the lake in the grounds. Interestingly Charles, who later succeeded to the estate, became an enthusiastic sailor. In the winter months the family migrated southwards to their old home – Lulworth Castle. Indeed, many winters were spent on the continent, at resorts which included Leghorn, Lucerne and Boulogne.

To his own Roman Catholic religious community he was a generous benefactor. A frequent expression of his was:

> I have received this estate as a special gift of God, and it is fitting that I should devote more than an ordinary share of it to his service.

As a county magistrate he also fulfilled a civic role, and in 1852 he held the office of High Sheriff of Lancashire.

Charles Weld-Blundell

> One of the most interesting local politicians was Mr. Charles Weld-Blundell, Lord of the Manor of Birkdale. In his early days he fought Preston as a Liberal, but as he matured he cried a plague on both your houses and became a critic of politicians generally. Towards the close of his life he made a feature of addressing his tenants in the Cambridge Hall and for out-spokenness there has been nothing to equal these addresses.
> *The Southport Journal*, 28th September 1934.

Unlike his father, Charles Weld-Blundell was not content to enjoy the life of a country gentleman, whilst keeping a watchful eye on the profitable development of Birkdale. He married in 1884 and was already 42 when, three years later, he inherited the estates. Educated at Stonyhurst and Christ Church, Oxford, a brief military career had been prematurely terminated when an accident prevented him from riding, an insurmountable handicap for a young officer in the Fourth Hussars. Subsequently, like many contemporaries, he travelled extensively. Indeed he was in the Transvaal when his father died in 1887.

These years of waiting appear to have made him somewhat restless and imbued him with a sense of urgency. There is evidence to suggest that he had taken some part in the management of the Birkdale Estate at least as early as 1874, and on succeeding his father, he immediately plunged into quite contentious schemes. The estate had been tardy in meeting its obligations in respect of roads and sewers and relationships with the Local Board were not cordial, but he did try to improve this situation with the gift of a clock for the town hall tower.

His new responsibilities as a landowner did not diminish his interest in politics. He unsuccessfully stood as a candidate in County Council and Parliamentary elections. His allegiances were very loosely with the Liberals, although he was an implacable opponent of many of this party's policies. He was a man of strongly held and somewhat idiosyncratic political views.

He frequently used gatherings of his tenants as an opportunity to air his views. In 1908 he entertained over 700 of his tenants at Ince Blundell. The festivities included cricket, dancing, boating, and, of course, feasting. Time was also found, however, for the squire to launch a vigorous attack on the Education Bill and the Licensing Bill, which were currently before the House of Commons. Weld-Blundell described the former as ". . . thorough cant". In regard to intemperance, he remarked: ". . . there is no more danger in drinking beer than in mutton chops taken in excess." More controversial was a highly sectarian statement in which he entreated his tenants not to vote for Nonconformist candidates. He argued that the radicals and their Nonconformist following were dangerous enemies of their country.[3]

A fervent Roman Catholic, Charles Weld-Blundell's religious beliefs appear to have been as idiosyncratic and passionately held as were his political views. Here again he seized the opportunities afforded by public platforms to air his views, including launching attacks on the Catholic hierarchy.

During the 1890s Weld-Blundell was seldom seen in Birkdale. The family regularly wintered at Lulworth Castle, and he appeared to be spending more time at his London town house – Blundell House, Campden Hill, Kensington. Lord Derby judged that Charles was ". . . something of a scholar and artist, having cultivated tastes and literary knowledge."[4] His letters were laden with classical allusions and he undoubtedly entertained literary ambitions, which found some expression in his publication of a London-based journal – *The Englishman*. Of local interest he promoted the *Birkdale Pioneer* for, he claimed, the benefit of the people in his estates at Birkdale and Ainsdale. Critics suggested that this "little journal" was merely a vehicle for the airing of Weld-Blundell's views and pushing his personal interests. Started in November 1909, it was expensively produced on glossy paper. Illustrated with photographs, it had the style of a nineteenth-century *Lancashire Life*, but without advertisements. Weld-Blundell did not regard it as a money-making venture, and in fact it lost some £2,500 before it closed in the following August.

Weld-Blundell appeared to relish confrontation. He was ever ready to have recourse to the courts to defend what he believed to be his rights. He also understood the advantage conferred by his considerable wealth – he was able to threaten legal action and thus challenge less wealthy opponents, including Birkdale's local authority, to risk the possible high cost of failure. Despite advice from one judge to avoid further litigation he, or the Estate, were regularly involved. It is tempting to speculate that, as well as entertaining literary ambitions, Weld-Blundell was also a frustrated lawyer. Indeed, following one trivial incident he chose to conduct his own case. He had been driving a coach and four in Maghull when it was in collision with a motor wagon, which he contended was travelling at more than the permitted five miles-per-hour. The wagon driver countered by asserting that Weld-Blundell had no more control of his coach than the man in the moon; nevertheless, he was found guilty and fined.

Although he spent more of his time in London and the day-to-day running of the Estate rested with the local agent, Weld-Blundell continued to exercise a major influence on the Township. The necessary contacts between the estate and the local authority were cool, frequently resulting in acrimony and even litigation. Weld-Blundell's acceptance of an invitation to become Chairman of the Birkdale Council during 1903, the Coronation year, brought only a temporary thaw in this relationship.

NEW BIRKDALE: ITS LOCAL GOVERNMENT

North Meols Parish Vestry Highway Board 1835–1863

> Rapidly increasing its inhabited areas, in defiance of its swamps and morasses, its magnanimous indifference to drains and sewers and such like unpleasant subjects, and its nightly darkness. Strange indeed that it continues without Local Government.
> *Southport Visiter*, 14th March 1862

As a part of the Parish of North Meols, Old Birkdale had been under the jurisdiction of the parish vestry, administered from distant Churchtown, for such little local government as existed. North Meols was one of the few parishes in England to take advantage of the General Highways Act of 1835 and set up a Highways Board, which was in effect a committee of the parish vestry, responsible for roads only. In Birkdale tension grew between this farmer-dominated group, which met at the schoolroom on the Common, and the incoming residents of Birkdale Park who, although providing an increasing proportion of the rates, had little say in how the money was spent. At a protest meeting in 1863 it was pointed out that the Board had spent £127 on roads in Birkdale Park against £181 in the thinly populated farming district, whilst the rates paid in the Park were £266 compared with only £97 on the other side of the railway line.

An Improvement Act of 1846 had already freed the new residential/resort town of Southport from the control of the parish vestry, and led to the establishment of Improvement Commissioners, with wide-ranging responsibilities. The residents of Birkdale Park were agitating for the reform of local government in their part of the parish also.

At a meeting with Local Government Commissioners, in 1863, residents of the Park argued that the interests of the farmers were not those of Birkdale Park and should be separately handled. There was a fear that the farmers would be too much under the control of the agent of the landlord. It was claimed that as many farms were let by the year, the resulting insecurity of tenure ensured that the farmers voted as directed by the landowner. There was a feeling among the suburban residents of Birkdale Park that they would be best served by a Board of their own, or perhaps by amalgamation with Southport. Despite the entreaties of the Birkdale Park residents, however, the outcome of the Commission's deliberations was a Local Government Act which placed the whole Township of Birkdale in the hands of a Board of Commissioners.

Birkdale Local Board 1863–1894

> Among the multitudinous governing bodies of this much governed country, not a few seem bent on showing the very small amount of wisdom which passes for administrative purposes. In that respect the Birkdale Local Board appears to be quite a model, judging by the report of their last meeting.
>
> *The London Globe*, June 1889

Party politics played no part in the early years of the Birkdale Local Board. The question of amalgamation with Southport appears to have been the only issue, and the majority opposed it.

Weld-Blundell's influence on the new Board was soon apparent. For its seal, the Board adopted the arms of Weld-Blundell, around which were printed the words: "Birkdale Local Government Board 1863". James Blundell, a farmer and understeward to the Lord of the Manor, had been surveyor for the old Highways Board and was appointed surveyor for the new Board. There were occasions when Fisher, Weld-Blundell's agent, did not only attend meetings of the Board but was allowed to speak. Indeed, in a discussion on amalgamation, he told the Board that ". . . on the day that Birkdale amalgamated with Southport, property would depreciate by 50%".[5] After several stormy meetings the minority on the Board favouring amalgamation was defeated.

Political power in Birkdale moved from the farmers on the Common to the new residents of the Park, leading a contemporary to comment that: "The Board is representative of the monied section only."[6] Having gained control of the Township, Birkdale Park residents quickly came to favour the notion of an independent Birkdale. With amalgamation off the agenda elections were no longer contested and the Board made nominations to fill any vacancies. The Birkdale Local Board seemed to subscribe to the "He who governs least, governs best" school of local administration.

The Birkdale Board was not extravagant, and its principal policy aim appeared to be to set a rate at a level lower than that obtaining in Southport, and thus make it attractive to residents. The major item of expenditure was the cost of making roads.

Relationships between the local administrations in Birkdale and Southport were always fraught. Acrimony characterised all the necessary exchanges between these neighbours. Southport supplied Birkdale with gas, making an extra charge for Birkdale consumers as, unlike Southport ratepayers, they bore none of the capital and management costs. Discussion of Birkdale's dissatisfaction with its gas supply dominated many meetings of the Local Board. Complaints about poor illumination were legion. Perhaps the most amusing came from Thomas Docksey, one of several councillors who were members of Birkdale Golf Club. He told the Council that on the previous ". . . Saturday evening at the golf house they had three gas lights burning, but even then it was impossible to read the scores without the aid of candles."[7]

Birkdale's political apathy only appeared to be disturbed when the township was threatened by schemes involving increased expenditure, or by amalgamation and the bogey of having to subsidise Southport's more ambitious approach to local government. In 1871, however, the Board had to fund a comprehensive sewerage scheme to overcome a problem that was already threatening the residential viability of Birkdale, and was to be the issue which dominated the Township and eventually determined the amalgamation issue. Here action, and its consequent expense, was imperative.

Despite this activity, elections to the Board were infrequent and the members knew that the real power in Birkdale was economic and rested with the wealthy ratepayers of Birkdale Park. The Township could not afford to alienate them and thus to lose the substantial contribution they made to the rates. These ratepayers were equally aware of their power and exercised it through deputations and petitions to the Board. One such petition caused a member to state that: ". . . emanating as it did from such an influential body of ratepayers it demands our most careful consideration."[8]

A further attempt by Southport to bring about amalgamation, in 1876, was successfully resisted and the Birkdale Park residents were able to continue to enjoy the lower domestic rates and social seclusion of Birkdale along with the facilities of adjoining Southport.

With the spectre of amalgamation again banished, the Board returned to its slumbers – meetings were short, and reports of proceedings were frequently very brief, or even absent. A correspondent wrote that: "The ruling power of the Township is a most inert machine, a do little machine, . . . Keeping roads seems a Herculean strain."[9]

The Council is drifting away from the representative system and is, in the mind of both parties, tending itself to the suspicion that attaches to a bureaucracy.

Southport Visiter, 4th June 1908

Under the provisions of the Local Government Act of 1894, Birkdale became an Urban District of Lancashire and a new Council had to be elected. One of the first acts of the Council was to procure a new seal. Perhaps an indication of the changed relationship between the local authority and the landowner was the fact that it did not incorporate the arms of Weld-Blundell.

For the first time Birkdale was divided into wards, thus giving political strength to the rapidly expanding working-class population inland of the railway. Nevertheless the reality of Birkdale politics continued to be that: "He who pays the piper calls the tune." Birkdale Park contained only a fifth of Birkdale's houses, but provided almost half of the Township's rates. These wealthy ratepayers had no wish to see the introduction of schemes which would disturb the residential tranquillity of Birkdale Park, nor did they want municipal expenditure beyond that which was essential to maintain this peaceful suburb. The Council was a clique, based on "accommodation" between councillors from both the Liberal and Conservative parties. Elections were normally only fought when a sitting councillor, from either party, decided not to continue, otherwise they were returned unopposed. The majority of councillors now lived east of the railway line, in a new middle-class area in and around Liverpool Road. The wealthier residents of Birkdale Park had learned that they did not have to sit on the Council in order to exercise power.

Beyond providing roads and necessary sewerage facilities, there had been little in the way of municipal enterprise. In 1902, Birkdale's loans were only a quarter of those which the national Local Government Board would have allowed it to borrow, a position enjoyed by very few authorities. The Council's low-key approach to local government had been matched by the attitude of its gout-ridden Law Clerk, John Smallshaw, who had served it for 40 years. A councillor described him as ". . . a man in a thousand in trying to keep down expenses."[10] Birkdale favoured private enterprise rather than municipal ventures. The Council did not provide its own gas, water, or electricity; it had no cemetery, market, library, or art gallery; whilst, as will be seen, Victoria Park, Rotten Row and the Esplanade had been financed by a railway company.

About the turn of the century, for reasons that are difficult to discern, the Council adopted a relatively more ambitious approach to local government. Money was spent for purposes other than roads and sewers. In addition, the Council suddenly seemed to be aware of its image. It appears that J.F. Keeley, the Board's principal officer, contributed substantially to this initiative. In 1899,

18

Birkdale U.D.C. inaugural Chairman's Sunday in 1907.

Birkdale Carnegie Library Book Plate.

19

he produced the first of the Council's comprehensive Year Books and illustrated guides. A new coat of arms for the township was introduced. Although not including the Weld-Blundell crest, it was based on the arms of the old barony of Blundell, which had become extinct in the fourteenth century. The motto "A Bonis ad Meliora" represented an optimistic view of the Township's future – "From good things to better ones".

In tune with this higher profile approach to municipal stewardship, a deputation to Lulworth Castle in 1902 successfully persuaded Weld-Blundell to accept the Chairmanship of the Council in Coronation year. Many local authorities asked local landowners to accept civic office in this year of celebration. In neighbouring Southport the major landowner, Mr. Charles Scarisbrick, was Mayor. Weld-Blundell, a staunch royalist, had recently entertained King Edward at Lulworth Castle. He shared with the king a passion for yachting, and His Majesty had arrived at Lulworth Cove in his yacht. Weld-Blundell donated £50 to the township's Coronation Festivities Fund, and planted a commemorative chestnut tree in Victoria Park. To mark the occasion the Council distributed 3,000 silver coated medals, bearing Birkdale's coat of arms. Although the Coronation was the pretext for the Council's invitation to Weld-Blundell to become Chairman, there was a hope that the gesture would help to heal the rift which had developed between it and the landowner. A member of the delegation explained that the presence of the Lord of the Manor in the Council would enable him to ". . . acquire a much more intimate knowledge of the affairs of the community."[11] Unfortunately a severe attack of pneumonia restricted his attendances to two meetings, for one of which he arrived late. Nevertheless, evidence of a more cordial relationship was soon apparent. Weld-Blundell acknowledged that it was a long time since he had done anything for Birkdale, and he offered the Council a site for a library, along with £1,000 with which to build it.

Despite increased borrowing to support the recent bout of Council activity, Weld-Blundell rightly pointed out that Birkdale was remarkable for the small size of its debt. The contrast with the position in Southport was dramatic. Southport had been a very active authority, and although it had accumulated large debts it had also acquired a wealth of public assets. The Council owned tramways, a gas undertaking, public parks, a marine lake, a Science and Art School, an art gallery and public libraries, meteorological and astronomical observatories, a drill hall, markets, public slaughter houses, a town hall and a concert hall.

Amalgamation of Birkdale and Southport: The Final Solution

Brighton and Hove occupy positions analogous to those occupied by Southport and Birkdale. They are separated from each other by an imaginary line, and they are not as amicably disposed towards each other as they might be.

Southport Visiter, 11th April 1899

The local press parodied Southport's persistent, but unsuccessful, amalgamation approaches to Birkdale as the actions of a spurned suitor. Nevertheless, amalgamation again became a live issue early in the twentieth century. Southport had a particularly strong motive for such a move at this time. At the census of 1901, its population was still below that required for County Borough status, which would give it enhanced local government powers. The absorption of Birkdale would enable it to achieve the necessary population level. In 1902, a dialogue between the two authorities eventually occurred. Representatives from the two councils sat down together in a series of confidential meetings to consider the feasibility of amalgamation.

In his *Municipal Recollections*, J.E. Jarratt, the Town Clerk of Southport, reveals that protracted negotiations got as far as a discussion of terms of amalgamation. It was at this point that a deputation of Birkdale Park residents appeared at a crucial meeting of the Birkdale Council. This group included some of Birkdale's largest and thus most influential ratepayers, and had the backing of a petition bearing some 500 signatures. These memorialists had one purpose: to preserve the quiet high-class residential character of Birkdale Park. One argued that Southport had ". . . an apparently increasing disposition to run that town in the interests of excursionists and day trippers."[12] This, he insisted, threatened the character of Birkdale and the property there. The intervention was sufficient to cool the ardour of the temporarily adventurous Birkdale councillors. Birkdale Council summarily broke off the contacts, with a resolution that:

> . . . having given the most careful consideration to the proposals submitted by Southport, the Council do not consider they contain any sufficient inducements that could justify them to change the existing state of affairs.[13]

Southport seized upon the wording of this resolution which suggested that it was only the terms which had been offered that had forestalled agreement. The Southport Council contended that the terms were adequate, and that it was willing to submit them for the judgement of the appropriate authority. Accordingly, it applied to the Local Government Board for an order to amalgamate the two townships.

Once again there was an Inquiry with all the major parties being legally represented. The Southport case for amalgamation was as follows: that Birkdale was a suburb of Southport, with the boundaries dividing them being entirely arbitrary; that as a suburb it relied on Southport for shops, and places of entertainment; that Birkdale had no art gallery or public library; and that Southport and Birkdale could be more economically managed by a single authority. There were also complaints about the efficiency of the Birkdale sewerage system which, it was alleged, had contaminated water courses running through Southport.

Charles Weld-Blundell opposed amalgamation with Southport. He favoured the bringing together of Birkdale, Ainsdale and Formby: he was the sole landowner of the first two and owned part of the latter. For several years he had actively promoted Ainsdale as a seaside residential town and entertained visions of a continuous settlement, on Weld-Blundell property, under a single municipal authority. He wrote to the Birkdale Council telling them that they could only stave off amalgamation if:

> We have embedded ourselves already with all the other townships between Southport and the sea (or Southern Hills) both of them being similar towns in aims and character and closely contiguous for mutual aid in population and support to enable us to be erected into a County Borough.[14]

He went on to suggest that vanity could be their ally: ". . . there are some I worr of at Formby who would not at all object to a chance of Aldermanic robes, or a Mayor's chain of office." In an attempt to secure his scheme he vigorously lobbied representatives from the three communities. He, in turn, was lobbied by Jarratt, on behalf of Southport. Weld-Blundell's files contain a confidential letter in which Jarratt made a sensational offer to Weld-Blundell: Southport would finance extending its Promenade from Southport to Ainsdale, with the possibility of an electric tramway.

> This would, I think you will agree with me, materially assist the development not only of your seafront (at Ainsdale), but also of the land on such roads as you might think proper to make at right angles and parallel to the sea.[15]

This tempting inducement, not mentioned in Jarratt's later account in his *Municipal Recollections*, was sufficient to persuade Weld-Blundell to meet a deputation from Southport. Jarratt reports that, at this meeting, Weld-Blundell was inclined to agree with the Southport proposal and promised to put his views in writing, but did not do so.

At the Inquiry, Weld-Blundell was represented by F.E. Smith, later Lord Birkenhead, but then a young barrister. Jarratt told Smith of his discussion with Weld-Blundell, and Smith agreed with the pro-amalgamation view which Jarratt said Weld-Blundell held. Jarratt reports that this was contrary to the instructions Smith had received, but without seeking confirmation from Weld-Blundell's solicitor, Smith seized the first opportunity to make a short statement supporting amalgamation as being in the best interests of Weld-Blundell's estate. On the surface this act might suggest arrogant incompetence on Smith's part. The 'Southport sweetener' offered to Weld-Blundell must have been very tempting and perhaps we do not know the full story. What is certain is that immediately after making this statement, and without seeing Weld-Blundell's solicitor,

Smith returned to London. Thus for this Inquiry the Estate was supporting amalgamation.

Birkdale had prepared itself for the fray by spending £3,000 of its reserves to keep the rates down in this crucial year. The Council had also held a plebiscite on amalgamation, which secured a 75% response. These ratepayers registered a massive 82% vote against amalgamation. Armed with these statistics, Counsel for the Council argued that Birkdale did not want amalgamation, a proposition which Southport, however, was able to negate by pointing to the fact that Birkdale had actively negotiated amalgamation with Southport, and had only withdrawn because the terms offered had not been deemed sufficiently attractive.

Ironically, the outcome was not determined by the attitude of the landowner, or that of Birkdale's Council and residents. Once again the central role was played by sewage. Southport complained about the fouling of Fine Jane's Brook by the discharge from Birkdale's sewerage works, a long-standing bone of contention. Over the years Birkdale had spent considerable sums of money trying to remedy this situation. To Southport's acute embarrassment W.T. Bulpit, the vicar of Crossens, appeared before the Inquiry and he, in turn, complained bitterly about the sewage effluent that Southport discharged into the Crossens Channel, thus fouling that area. With its own sewerage system being shown to be inadequate, Southport was in no position to argue it should also take over responsibility for that of Birkdale, and Southport's bid to force amalgamation failed.

The relationships beween the two townships had been further complicated by their dealings with Ainsdale. The small village of Ainsdale was Birkdale's southern neighbour on the coastal strip, the next station down the line. Although linked by rail and road, Ainsdale village was, however, well detached from Birkdale. On several occasions in the past Ainsdale had broached the question of amalgamation with Birkdale. Such propositions appeared to have little advantage for Birkdale, and were rebuffed. Even Weld-Blundell's grandiose schemes for the development of a seaside residential town at Ainsdale were still more shadow than substance, and were not at the point where they could deliver sufficient rateable value to justify the cost of linking Ainsdale to Birkdale's public utilities. Nevertheless, prior to the hearing of the Birkdale Amalgamation Inquiry, Southport entered into amalgamation negotiations with Ainsdale and a provisional agreement was quickly achieved. The absorption of Ainsdale would have given Southport only a modest increase in population, but much more significantly it would have left Birkdale an island flanked on two sides by Southport. "Learning of this intrigue", the Birkdale Council recognised its potential vulnerability and immediately opened negotiations with Ainsdale.[16] The previously rejected suitor was now enthusiastically wooed. Birkdale's hastily assembled dowry included the inducement of a highly preferential rate for Ainsdale, subsidised by Birkdale ratepayers. It also contained the promise to provide a sewerage system for Ainsdale within six months following amalgamation. Not surprisingly this generous offer was accepted with alacrity. Although the two townships were not formally united until 1905, Birkdale had thwarted Southport's clever ploy to encircle it before the hearing of the Amalgamation Inquiry. The promise to deliver a sewerage system had, however, set the clock running on the time-bomb which was to contribute to Birkdale's later disappearance as an independent township.

The Birkdale Council's sewerage system for Ainsdale was to be linked to the necessary improvement of its own facilities. The plan was to join Birkdale's sewerage system to one to be built in Ainsdale; to build new sewerage works to service both; and to provide a waste outfall on the foreshore, at the southern margin of Ainsdale. The Local Government Board was responsible for sanctioning the necessary loan and the scheme would have to satisfy it on two counts: technical efficiency in relation to cost, and environmental impact. The obvious weakness was the location of the waste outfall to the south of Ainsdale. This caused concern both to Weld-Blundell, who was attempting to develop Ainsdale-on-Sea as a seaside residential resort, and the Southport Council which saw the proposed outlet as a health threat to its holiday beach.

The Birkdale Council's negotiations with its consultant engineers, the landowner, and the Local Government Board were shrouded in secrecy. A further fundamental problem of the scheme was that it was attempting to work against the natural gravitation of the district. The land fell to the north, but Birkdale's sewage would have to be pumped to the south, through progressively deeper sewers. Delay followed on delay as schemes were amended in an attempt to meet the requirements of the Local Government Board. As the scheme became more complicated the estimated costs escalated. It was these figures that the Council was anxious to hide from Southport and from its own ratepayers. The Council publicly persisted in its claim that the cost would be only £25,000, a figure which did not, however, include essential future extensions which would increase the real cost to £72,000.

By 1910, the clock on Birkdale's sewage time-bomb had run out. Although Southport had been embarrassed by the exposure of the inadequacy of its own sewerage system at the Amalgamation Inquiry of 1903, it had moved quickly to put its house in order and had built a new sewerage works at Crossens. Southport was now in a position to offer to the Local Government Board an alternative sewerage scheme, which would cater for Birkdale and Ainsdale at a cost of only £36,170. Its new sewerage works would discharge all the waste into the Ribble Channel. As this scheme was acceptable to the Local Government Board, which had rejected Birkdale's latest submission, amalgamation now appeared to be inevitable.

Completely boxed in, the Birkdale Council was reconciled to the inevitability of amalgamation and quickly agreed terms with Southport. These included a reduction of 6d in the rates (which were then by that amount higher than the rates in Southport) and the removal of the historical differential in the charge for gas. The matter was put to a plebiscite of Birkdale's ratepayers and some 85% responded. Of these 2,229 voted for amalgamation and only 380 against. With the authorities of both Southport and Birkdale now supporting amalgamation, there was little doubt about the outcome of the Local Government Board Inquiry. Nevertheless, the Inspector asked about the attitude of the landowner. In answer, Weld-Blundell's counsel replied: "I am supporting, sir, and quite prepared to act as father to give Birkdale away to be married with Southport" (laughter). Birkdale, so long the coy maiden rejecting the overtures of her Southport suitor, was finally led to the altar of amalgamation on All Fools' Day, 1912.

CHAPTER THREE

BIRKDALE PARK 1848–1874: THE BIRTH OF A SUBURB

The buildings are generally on a scale of grandeur and magnificence superior to those of Southport, and many of them are occupied by opulent merchants and manufacturers from Liverpool and Manchester, as well as by other wealthy and highly respectable persons.

Mannex Directory, 1866

WAS JOHN AUGHTON THE FOUNDER?

Edward Kemp's 1848 plan for Birkdale Park was an ambitious design for a seaside garden town. Not previously published, this plan showed spacious middle-class residences laid out in an elegant landscape, complete with crescents and esplanades. Thomas Weld-Blundell was closely involved in the presentation. Estate papers show that it was on his insistence that two 'views' of the proposed development were incorporated in the top corners of the plan.[1] After seeing a draft he wanted the illustrations changed to show villas of a superior quality. Plans such as this were produced as promotional literature, and were not blue-prints. If a landowner wanted to ensure that development followed the plan precisely, he had to be prepared to fund it, and not leave its fate to market forces. Thomas Weld-Blundell was not a wealthy landowner at this time, and having incurred considerable legal expenses to secure his estate, he wanted to keep his speculation to a minimum. Indeed, it appears that he had to negotiate a loan to fund his development of Birkdale.[2] Initial expenses were restricted to Kemp's fee, the cost of advertising, and later the cost of road building. His solicitor suggested that he was prepared to spend £5,000 on roads and sewers. In the event little road building took place until the leaseholders had paid their share for half of the carriage way fronting onto their property. Indeed, the *Southport Visiter* later suggested that the lack of builders taking up Weld-Blundell leases was ". . . because there were no roads, and the wild sandhills did not appear to be such an eligible investment as, with a little

Edward Kemp's 1848 Plan of Birkdale Park.

27

expense, they could be made."[3] Not for Weld-Blundell the risk of massive spending on moulding the environment, in order to try to attract residents.

The initial advertisement offering leases had appeared in the *Southport Visiter* on 31st September 1848. Further advertisements were placed in Liverpool, Preston, Wigan, Bolton, Blackburn and Manchester papers. On the 22nd September 1849, the *Southport Visiter* reported that ". . . agreements were negotiated, building plans prepared and a building society ready to construct a park with villas in Birkdale." Papers from the office of Weld-Blundell's solicitor confirm the existence of such a scheme. They include a much amended draft lease, dated 2nd February 1849, for a Mr. John Jones of Liverpool.[4] It was for 30 acres of "waste" land on the east side of the road leading out of Southport in a southerly direction (Lulworth Road). The lease states that Weld-Blundell intended to form an ornamental garden – Blundell Square – next to "the strand of the sea" and that Jones would have to pay towards its upkeep. The houses were to be of at least £500 in value, a clear indication that this was to be a high-class development.

Weld-Blundell had realised that his best opportunity for development was on the fringe of Southport, where similar development in Liverpool Road (now Lord Street West) had previously come to an abrupt and artificial end at the boundary line. The road was sealed by a gated fence, thus creating a cul-de-sac – an arrangement approved by the late Mr. Charles Blundell. From as early as 1846, Thomas Weld-Blundell had been in communication with the Scarisbrick Estate in an attempt to have the gate opened, on the grounds that it was a public road. It was not in the commercial interest of the Scarisbrick Estate to assist the opening up of rival building land, and they prevaricated. Weld-Blundell had to threaten legal action before access was finally gained.[5]

Weld-Blundell also appreciated the importance to a suburb of access to the railway. On the 22nd June 1849 the *Southport Visiter* reported speculation that Weld-Blundell had offered the Liverpool, Crosby and Southport Railway Company the land to make a branch line to the boundary of Birkdale and Southport at Lulworth Road. The offer included land for a station and a large hotel. Such a development would certainly have given a "kick start" to Birkdale Park. Credibility is added to this story with the newspaper reporting the placing of surveying flags to mark the route. It seems, however, that in 1849 this branch line was a victim of an agreement, by which the Lancashire and Yorkshire Railway Company was proposing to buy the Liverpool, Crosby and Southport Company. An unfortunate by-product of the failure to build this branch line appears to have been Jones' decision not to proceed with his plans in Birkdale. He abandoned the venture in favour of an "attractive site in Cheshire." Although not built, the proposed branch line found its way onto some copies of a contemporary Ordnance Survey map. Some historians have accepted this map as evidence that a passenger line and station were built, others have thought that it showed a line to remove sand prior to house building.[6] There is, however, no concrete evidence to support either view.

In order to realise Weld-Blundell's urban ambitions, builders with capital to invest had to come forward. The first to do so was John Aughton.

John Aughton had worked with his father Richard, under the famous architect Decimus Burton, on Peter Fleetwood-Hesketh's financially ill-fated attempt to develop Fleetwood as a watering place and a major ferry port for Ireland and Scotland. Aughton, who had lived in Preston, came to Southport in the 1840s. There is the possibility that this move was a result of his link with the Hesketh family, through his work in Fleetwood. Perhaps he was returning to his roots, since his father was born in Churchtown. Or possibly he just recognised the potential for a builder in this rapidly growing resort. Whatever the reasons, his first major commission in Southport appears to have been the building of the Congregational Chapel, which he started in 1846.

Of Birkdale Park we are told by Bland, in his *Annals of Southport*, that on 8th August, 1850, "The first stones were laid for Lulworth House, Mr. John Aughton being the builder." This is confirmed in a brief manuscript history of the Weld-Blundell Family in the Estate papers.[7] Strangely, there is no evidence of the presence of this or any other new building in Birkdale Park in the 1851 census. This national census would have been undertaken with great care and enumerators were required to include houses which were still being built.

Bland also tells us that in the same year, 1850, Aughton started a second house, 'Birkdale Lodge', on a nearby plot. The lease required him to build a "substantial dwelling house" to the value of £700. Greenwood, in his *Thatch, Towers and Colonnades*, suggests that Aughton, or his architect, set a vernacular style, with a strong Italian influence, for many of the great houses built in Birkdale Park, and that 'Birkdale Lodge' is one of the best examples of this style.

It was the erection of these, and other houses in Birkdale Park, that gave rise to the legend that John Aughton was the founder of Birkdale. Although Aughton was the first to build on one of Weld-Blundell's plots, it was Thomas Weld-Blundell who had conceived the scheme and who was, therefore, the founder. Aughton's initiative was that of a commercial builder seeking to extend his operations. The accounts of Weld-Blundell's solicitor contain inconclusive evidence about Aughton having received a loan to fund his building.[8] Records of the Southport Improvement Commissioners show that he was also actively engaged, at this time, on a number of housebuilding projects in Southport.

The relationship between Aughton and the Estate quickly deteriorated. In 1853, he was being pressed to honour his covenants and to contribute to the making of Aughton Road. He was also under pressure to pay for damage which, it was alleged, he had done to "sods and soil" in Aughton Road, and for

'Birkdale Lodge', Lulworth Road.

rent which he owed. The figure involved was about £130, and there was a possibility of the forfeiture of leases which he held. It seems that he had the leases for fourteen houses, including some on the sea front.

In 1854 he emigrated to Canada, in order to undertake a contract on the Grand Canadian Trunk Railway. His friends organised a farewell dinner for him at the Victoria Hotel. In his speech Aughton revealed that he had come to Southport in order:

> . . . to make an investment of capital, I began at Southport, and a short time afterwards I threw my efforts into the neighbouring village or town of Birkdale . . . In doing good to Birkdale I felt I was doing good to Southport.

James Hunt, the proprietor of Southport's Scarisbrick Hotel, enthusiastically declared that:

> I do not believe that there would have been a single brick or stone laid in Birkdale Park had it not been for him, to this day.[9]

This remark was a suitable valedictory statement from a friend on a festive occasion, but it cannot be thought to be a serious historical judgement. If

Aughton had not built, others would, at some point, have taken advantage of Weld-Blundell's decision to open up the area for building. Nevertheless, it is possible that it was this quotation that has helped to build the view that John Aughton was the founder of Birkdale. It was an opinion shared by other contemporaries: in 1856 the Rector, the Rev. Charles Hesketh, referred to Aughton as "... the founder of this new magnificent and flourishing place."[10]

During Aughton's absence his business interests in Birkdale were handled by his solicitor, and it was during this period that his debt to the Estate was settled. After a relatively short stay in Canada, he returned from those "... inhospitable and frozen regions" in December 1856.

Back in Birkdale, he set about building a house for himself in Aughton Road, a road whose name was to serve as a permanent reminder of the unique contribution he had made in building Birkdale Park's first house. As before, he continued to have contractual problems with both the Estate and individuals for whom he built houses. Again his stay was brief. In 1857 he built new schoolrooms for Holy Trinity Church and the Temperance Institute in Southport, but thereafter little is known of his actions and even his whereabouts are unknown. He died in 1859, and it seems strange that someone whose earlier life had been so conspicuously public should make such an anonymous exit from the local scene.

THE BEGINNINGS: A HIGH-CLASS RESIDENTIAL SUBURB?

Kemp's original plan for Birkdale Park showed roads corresponding to Lulworth Road, Westcliffe Road and Weld Road. The first villas were built in Lulworth Road, close to the Southport boundary, but others were slow to follow. Much of the early demand was for cheaper dwellings suitable for the lower middle classes. Weld-Blundell's need to generate income meant that he could not afford to wait for purchasers for the more expensive villa plots to come forward. He had to take advantage of such selling opportunities as were available. It was in Aughton Road that the estate offered plots for cheaper houses. Although there was no indication of this development on Kemp's plan, it was here that much of the early building speculation occurred. The style was hardly in keeping with the landowner's ambitious initial intentions for the Park. The first lease, for number 2 on the south-west side, was issued on the 20th May 1851, to John Rimmer, a gardener. It was for a 5,000 square yard plot and allowed the building of two houses at a cost of only £125 each.[11] In the same year Bland reported that the Southport Oddfellows processed to Aughton Road "... to inspect some houses in the course of erection, the funds for them being advanced by the Society." By 1858, 54 of Birkdale Park's 99 occupied houses were in Aughton Road.

Although allowing relatively cheap houses to be built in Aughton Road, it appears that the estate was sensitive to their proximity to the higher-value villas. In October 1851, Weld-Blundell's solicitor wrote to John Rimmer instructing him ". . . to remove a bedroom in his house which looks into Lulworth Road or his lease would be treated as forfeited."[12] There was no attempt to maintain a high-class residential ethos in Aughton Road. It became a mixture of terraces, semi-detached houses and villas, including some which were quite substantial. Additional payments to the Estate could secure amendments to the original leases, including permission to erect further buildings. The plots were deep and, in some cases, houses were built to the rear of those fronting on to the road.

The development around John Aughton's house, which was built on a plot at the rear of 'Birkdale Lodge', on the north-east side of Aughton Road, probably best illustrates this opportunist attitude. Aughton was allowed to build workshops and sawmills behind his house. By 1861 his house and business had been taken over by John Southern, formerly of Tulketh Street. The

Southern Road cottages.

32

census shows that he employed eighteen men and five boys, and became Birkdale Park's premier builder. By this time Southern's Aughton Road plot had been heavily built on. In addition to his own house, there was a substantial semi-detached pair, and behind it Southern Road – a small terrace of six tiny cottages. Two of the occupants of the cottages were sawyers, one was a joiner, and there was one painter. In one of the other cottages a tailor lived with his wife and two children, in addition the couple had five lodgers, all joiners. There were two plasterers and a joiner lodging in the other cottages. It is possible that this terrace housed much of Southern's workforce, and on census night in 1861, there were 49 people living in nine dwellings, on a plot that might have been leased for one substantial villa.

Although the Estate was prepared to sacrifice standards in the granting of leases, it was diligent in insisting that leaseholders should meet the conditions of the covenants contained in them. In 1857 Edward Pedder was written to for building a second house in his yard without permission. Leaseholders were required to fence their property, and lay out flower gardens ". . . with all the usual and necessary plants, shrubs and trees." William Reid had obviously left his Aughton Road garden in a wild state and, in 1854, he was ordered to remove the indigenous willows and lay it out.[13] From the earliest days it was the residents who were charged with the responsibility of creating the garden suburb. Commercial gardeners were quick to see the potential, and George Davies took over at number 2 Aughton Road and ran a nursery. He also kept a museum of curiosities as an attraction for visitors.

Servant-keeping topped the list of middle-class "paraphernalia of gentility", and the number of servants in residence provided a tangible expression of social status.[14] Indeed, some people of quite modest income struggled to afford the expense of a single servant, usually a young girl in her first place. This ensured that at least the hostess didn't have to answer the door to admit visitors. The very act of keeping a servant allowed status-conscious residents to maintain appearances and to derive what have been described as ". . . the psychic benefits."[15] Nevertheless, in 1861 only a third of the Aughton Road households had resident servants, and only one, a schoolmaster Matthew Gibson, had more than one. Ten years later, approximately half of the residents kept a servant, but this was still not the profile of a high-class residential area. The Local Board *General Rate Book* for 1869 provides further objective evidence concerning Aughton Road. The average rent of £31 was much the lowest in Birkdale Park. Just under half of the houses had their rents assessed at under £25 a year. It was this figure that the government used as an indicator of whether families would use private or public elementary education. When the *Mannex Directory*, compiled in 1865, identified five of the six roads in the Park as being of the ". . . first order", it was significant that the one omitted from the list was Aughton Road.

BIRKDALE PARK: Estimated Annual Value of Rentals 1869

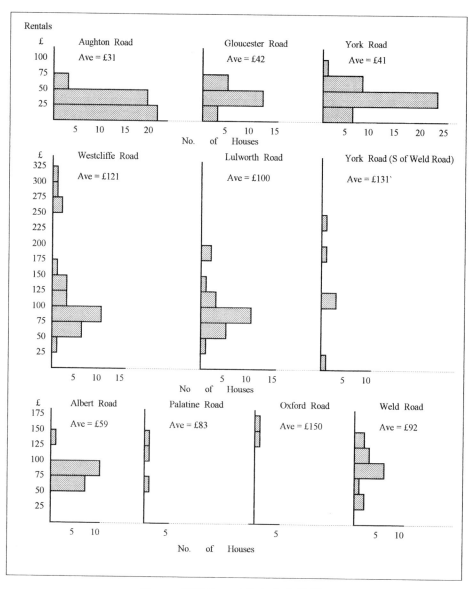

(Source: BLB General Rate Book 1869)

One possible reason for the failure of this part of Birkdale Park to develop along high-class residential lines was sabotage. Acts which had all the hallmarks of sabotage were, it was claimed, being committed by representatives of the Scarisbrick Estate, which still had many vacant plots in adjoining Southport. The townships were separated by the Boundary Brook, a tributary of the River Nile which meandered across the sands to join the sea. Although not physically imposing, it was these sluggish streams that had ". . .been the natural outlet of Birkdale's brooks since time immemorial."[16] The Nile was on Scarisbrick land in Southport, and the Scarisbrick Estate was accused by the editor of the *Southport Visiter* of damming up both the Boundary Brook and the Nile. The Scarisbrick Estate did not dispute the fact that the drains were being dammed, and Weld-Blundell referred the case to the Drainage Commissioners in London. He was told that he could compel the drain to be opened.[17] Any improvements he secured did not last, and as late as 1866 the charge was repeated in a report from Capt. Donnelly R.E. to the Privy Council.[18] This intermittent damming led to flooding, which in places attained a depth of two feet. The plots on the north-east side of Aughton Road ran ". . . in depth to an ancient watercourse (the Boundary Brook), including one half thereof."[19] Flooding in an area which was still dependent upon cess pits posed a considerable health hazard. Cess pits had strong local advocates. The houses were built on large plots, and these were deemed to have sufficient room for each to consume its own sewage. The porous nature of the sandy soil meant, however, that flooding threatened the water supply from the shallow domestic wells. The waterlogged conditions, which persisted into the 1860s, must have had an adverse effect on market values, and were only effectively countered when the Local Board installed sewers in the early 1870s.

The socially mixed development that Weld-Blundell allowed to occur in Aughton Road provided a buffer between Birkdale Park proper and Southport. By 1871 Talbot Street (later Hollybrook Road) had been built, but Southport was not interested in opening it up on its side. Vehicular access between the two townships was still limited to one narrow carriage way – now Lord Street West. Other links were restricted to footpaths. Aughton Road was marginal in every way.

From Aughton Road mixed development of very much the same kind continued south along York Road, with Gloucester Road providing a link to Lulworth Road.

The first lease in Gloucester Road, which was taken in 1853 by James Rimmer, another gardener, was the fourteenth in the Park. It was for a relatively small plot of just over 3,000 square yards. By 1857 there were ten houses, with plots varying in size between 4840 and 9680 square yards. Four years later there were nineteen. The Medical Officer confirmed that flooding, which occurred when the Boundary Brook was blocked, extended along

Hollybrook as far as Gloucester Road. In 1863, Isaac Thomas of 'Westwood House' complained that the neighbourhood was so wet he needed a flat bottomed boat. As late as 1869, 23 residents of Aughton Road and Gloucester Road presented a memorial to the Local Board claiming that their gardens and cellars were flooded in the winter, because of the closing of the main watercourse. It is interesting to note that, at that time, Gloucester Road had the lowest percentage of owner occupiers in Birkdale Park, with Aughton Road as its closest challenger. The mixture of property types reflected the uncertainty of social direction in the early days of Birkdale Park. The road contained nine detached villas, five semi-detached pairs, and a terrace of four modest houses – 'Arlington Place' – which later included Birkdale's first post office. This terrace absorbed part of an earlier farm building. Adjoining it, on the largest plot in the road, was 'Eskdale'. It is the presence of this large villa, built in 1871, that confirms that, after a shaky start, Birkdale Park was becoming a successful high-class residential area.

A change in social tone was evident from the occupations of the householders. In 1861, ten of the thirteen residents of Gloucester Road were retired men or women living on an income. The three in employment were a merchant, a schoolmaster and a gardener. By 1868, the *Johnson and Green Guide*

St. James' Church and "Castles in the Sand", c. 1860.

highlighted the emerging importance of the railway link with Liverpool, identifying seven of the eighteen householders as working there. They included: three merchants, a ship broker, an iron founder, an undertaker, a solicitor, and the assistant magistrates' clerk. In the same year Mary Holford, a portmanteau manufacturer who employed nineteen people, came to live in the road. The rents of six of the 21 houses were assessed at over £50, whilst there were only three at under £25.

Servant-keeping provides further evidence of these social changes. In 1861, only eight of the thirteen householders kept resident servants – seven had a single servant, whilst Henry Mathwin, a schoolmaster, had two. Ten years later there were eighteen houses with a total of 22 servants – eight households with one, and seven with two. The three houses without servants were those with rents below £25. One of them was an old cottage, which was reached by a passage at the back of 'Park Grove'. Assessed at only £8, it was occupied by a builder. The other two were the homes of early residents of the road – James Rimmer, the gardener and John Marsden, a retired inn-keeper from Chorley. The latter had apparently divided 'Orrell Villa', which he owned, to create two dwellings. In contrast, it was at the corner of Gloucester Road and Lulworth Road that John Fernley built his massive 'Clairville', where he was tended by a housekeeper, two housemaids and that token of affluence and status – a butler.

Villas in Lulworth Road were of a higher status than those in Gloucester Road, with an average rent of £100, but it appears that even there Thomas Weld-Blundell had been prepared to dilute his vision for Birkdale Park. John Fernley only agreed to take his 22,000 square yard plot after Weld-Blundell consented to give up his idea of erecting shops in Lulworth Road. Fernley regarded Birkdale Park as a suburb of Southport and was one of the early supporters of amalgamating it with Southport, rather than associating the Park with the Common. After a brief flirtation with Birkdale politics, he chose to use his "economic influence" as a major ratepayer, lobbying the authority on particular issues. Fernley was responsible for many acts of religious and civic philanthropy. It is perhaps significant that although he provided a Methodist church in Birkdale, the local social facilities for which he was responsible – the meteorological observatory in Hesketh Park, the drinking fountain and barometer on the Promenade for the fishermen, the land for the infirmary, and the bequest for a new lifeboat – were all located in Southport. He became a magistrate in Southport, and on several occasions acted as an intermediary between the feuding Southport and Birkdale local authorities.

Development on the plots facing the sea was in sharp contrast to that which occurred in Aughton Road, York Road, and Gloucester Road. Birkdale beach was backed by a small embankment, which provided prestigious sites for building. Here the development, if slow to happen, was in accord with Kemp's plan. Initially called West Cliff, and later Westcliffe, the road was in a premium

1861

	0	1	2	3	4	5	6+
Southern	6	-	-	-	-	-	-
Aughton	16	17	1	-	-	-	-
Hollybrook							
York	8	11	1	-	-	-	-
Gloucester	5	7	1	-	-	-	-
Albert							
Lulworth	-	2	6	3	1	-	-
Westcliffe	-	2	5	2	-	-	-
Palatine	-	1	-	-	-	-	-
Weld	-	3	1	-	-	-	-
Oxford							

1871

	0	1	2	3	4	5	6+
Southern	6	-	-	-	-	-	-
Aughton	20	19	4	1	-	-	-
Hollybrook	1	2	1	-	-	-	-
York	8	19	6	-	1	-	1
Gloucester	8	8	7	-	-	-	-
Albert	1	5	6	3	-	-	-
Lulworth	-	3	10	6	5	-	-
Westcliffe	-	2	7	8	2	2	-
Palatine	-	1	-	1	-	-	-
Weld	3	2	3	5	2	2	1
Oxford	-	-	-	1	-	1	-

1881

	0	1	2	3	4	5	6+
Southern	9	-	-	-	-	-	-
Aughton	20	22	8	2	-	-	-
Hollybrook	2	1	-	1	-	-	-
York	7	20	11	3	-	-	1
Gloucester	3	10	3	3	-	-	-
Albert	1	5	8	2	1	1	-
Lulworth	-	4	12	8	3	1	1
Westcliffe	-	3	10	9	5	2	2
Palatine	-	-	3	2	-	-	-
Weld	2	4	8	3	1	-	-
Oxford	-	-	2	2	-	2	1
Trafalgar	-	4	7	2	1	-	1
Grosvenor	-	1	5	-	1	-	1
Belgrave	-	3	1	1	-	-	-
Regent	-	2	5	-	-	-	-
Lancaster	-	1	2	-	-	-	-
Waterloo	-	-	-	2	-	-	1

1891

	0	1	2	3	4	5	6+
Southern	9	-	-	-	-	-	-
Aughton	11	20	7	4	-	-	-
Hollybrook	-	5	-	-	-	-	-
York	7	21	13	3	1	-	1
Gloucester	6	7	6	3	1	-	-
Albert	-	5	10	2	1	-	-
Lulworth	-	3	15	10	7	-	-
Westcliffe	-	2	7	8	3	1	1
Palatine	1	-	2	-	-	-	-
Weld	4	1	12	9	2	1	-
Oxford	-	1	9	5	5	1	-
Trafalgar	2	3	11	7	1	1	-
Grosvenor	-	4	4	4	2	1	-
Belgrave	2	7	4	1	-	-	-
Regent	-	5	6	3	-	-	-
Lancaster	-	1	11	2	-	-	-
Waterloo	-	1	3	5	1	-	1
Westbourne	-	4	4	1	-	-	-
Bickerton	-	7	3	2	-	-	-

Source: Census Enumerators' Returns

Birkdale Park: Servant-keeping 1861–1891.

position. Aughton held the leases at the Southport end of the road. An early resident was Holbrook Gaskell, a wealthy and relatively young retired engineer. In 1858, he moved into the spacious 'Wyborne Gate', opposite to 'Birkdale Lodge', close to the Southport boundary. His family, which included seven children, was looked after by an establishment of five resident servants. Like many Lancashire businessmen, Holbrook Gaskell was a staunch Unitarian,

Embankment overlooking the Beach in 1881.

and on discovering that there was no active congregation in the district he set about forming one. As the founder president of the Southport Unitarian Congregation, he was largely responsible for the building of their church in Portland Street. He was as radical in his politics as in his religion and was a very active supporter of the Liberal Party and of Gladstone, with whom he had a close personal link. The first Chairman of the Birkdale Local Board, Holbrook Gaskell became known as the "King of Birkdale". His reign was brief, and after leading the small minority favouring amalgamation with Southport he abdicated and concentrated his political energies in Southport, where he was influential in helping to secure its municipal incorporation. He became a magistrate and was president of the Convalescent Hospital.

The residents in the West Cliff Road houses overlooking the beach were to become known as the 'Frontagers'. The 1861 census lists houses on seven of these large plots. The *Johnson and Green* plan shows that seven years later there were sixteen. The highest value villas were those on the western side, between Beach Road and Weld Road. All these houses were assessed at rentals of over £200, whilst the average for the road was £121. A 'Frontager' whose name will be encountered frequently in the story of Birkdale was George Chamberlain, a Liverpool stockbroker, who lived at number 26 – 'Helensholme', a property on which he paid rates of £250 a year. He was an influential member of Birkdale Liberal Party and a substantial figure in the local Catholic community, but above all, he played a central role in several of the most important business enterprises in Birkdale.

Another 'Frontager', Mrs Ellen Burton, was an annuitant, living on unearned income, who was the resident at 'The Warren', a house on a four-acre site, which was valued at £10,000. There, this 40 year old widow, the daughter of a former chairman of the Lancashire and Yorkshire Railway Company, lived with her daughter, looked after by four resident servants. 'The Warren's' library contained over 3,000 books. One of Birkdale's grandees, Mrs. Burton was a strong supporter of St. James' Church and the Birkdale Conservative Association, to which she lent carriages on polling days. Her daughter could ride from 'The Warren's' stables, through a tunnel in the embankment at the bottom of the garden, to the beach.

The foreshore immediately in front of West Cliff Road was hardly salubrious. Although occasional high tides washed against this embankment, the beach was one of rough pasture, on which Weld-Blundell let out the grazing rights, and of large stagnant slimy lagoons, which gave off an abominable stench. These "dismal swamps" attracted repeated criticism and the Local Board's Health Committee made unsuccessful representations to Weld-Blundell, asking him to have the holes filled. There was no fashionable parade at the foot of the slope, although Birkdale people looked upon the sandy track ". . . as a sort of Rotten Row", which was popular with the township's equestrians.[20]

Weld-Blundell has rightly been given the credit for the quality of Birkdale's early roads. Unlike Southport, where the roads were surfaced with stone sets, those in Birkdale were asphalted. Following a demonstration, "Weld-Blundell called upon a new system developed by Mr Schrimshaw, who had pioneered a new form using pitch and tar and rollers."[21] This provided a smoother quiet surface and a drive around the new township became a popular carriage outing from Southport, much to the annoyance of the Park's residents, particularly the 'Frontagers'. Unfortunately, these roads had been cheaply constructed. In fact several of them had to be repaired before they could be dedicated for public use in 1855. The stone foundations were inadequate, and they were built without drains, thus providing a poor legacy for the Local Board, when it came to take them over.

The accurate street plan of Birkdale contained in the *Johnson and Green Guide*, published in 1868, shows that Birkdale Park between Aughton Road and Weld Road had been largely built up. The plan shows large plots and well spaced villas. It appears that it was more the influence of the market, rather than that of Weld-Blundell, which resulted in these standards being maintained. The appearance of the Park was greatly enhanced by the requirement that houses should be built fifteen yards back from the road. It was ironic that Weld-

Blundell's solicitor wanted to build a house in York Road only ten yards from the roadway. The Local Board rejected this proposal, which had been approved by Weld-Blundell, stating that it would set ". . . a bad example if he were to be the first to break through a practice which had proved judicious."[22] The Local Board also called the landowner to task over his plan to make Weld Road only 36 feet wide.[23]

Although Weld-Blundell had failed in his attempt to have a branch railway line built to serve the Lulworth Road area, Birkdale Station was moved, in 1851, from Birkdale Common to Weld Road, in order to serve Birkdale Park. Kemp's earlier plan shows it there, at the centre of the proposed development. It was claimed that early morning express trains offered Birkdale's commuters a journey time to Liverpool of only 35 minutes. The fact that the first houses in Birkdale Park were erected in Lulworth Road, alongside Southport, over a mile away from the new Birkdale Station, throws doubt on the significance of the railway as a major factor in the beginnings of Birkdale Park. During this period Weld-Blundell struggled with the directors of the railway company in an attempt to get express trains to stop at Birkdale. Southport contract holders

Horse-drawn tram.

41

were strongly opposed to this stop, as it added time to their journeys. Despite the building of the Park Hotel close to the station in 1859, there were only two houses at this end of Weld Road by 1868. The *Johnson and Green* plan shows that the station was still at the south-east margin of the built-up area. The horse-drawn tramway service, provided by the Southport Tramway Company, was to have its terminus at Birkdale Station, thus improving the transport situation within Birkdale Park. The line, which opened in 1873, ran to Churchtown, via Weld Road, York Road, Aughton Road, and then along Southport's Lord Street.

There was little link between the population of Birkdale Park and Old Birkdale. The 1861 and 1871 Census returns for Birkdale Park show only a handful of householders who had been born in Birkdale. All six lived in the socially mixed York Road. The best known was Cyrus Johnson, the former village schoolmaster. The others were two retired Birkdale farmers – James Carr and Robert Marshall – neither of whom kept a servant, and two locally born young grocers – Seth Rimmer and Isaac Blundell – who chose to ply their trade west of the railway. The sixth Birkdalian was Cornelius Blundell, a joiner. There were very few Birkdale Park residents who had even been born in other parts of North Meols, although just over half came from Lancashire.

Many of the early residents were retired men and spinsters or widows living on unearned income. In 1871, members of these groups comprised just under 40% of the householders. Almost half of them were to be found at the margins of the Park in Aughton Road and York Road. As development occurred deeper into the Park, the dwellings were of a superior kind. In 1869, the average rent in Albert (now Saxon) Road was £59, in Weld Road it was £92, whilst for the new houses beyond Weld Road it was over £100. An analysis of servant-keeping provides further evidence of this social profile. Houses without servants were found almost exclusively in Aughton Road, York Road and Gloucester Road. The three houses in Weld Road without servants were clustered around Goulder's stable yard, alongside the station. As Westcliffe Road, Lulworth Road and Weld Road were built up, more than half of the households had three or more servants. Only two houses aspired to a butler, although three had resident coachmen, and one a footman.

A rather odd intrusion into Birkdale Park's residential integrity was the Palace Hotel. When Weld-Blundell, or his agent, decided to allow a hotel within the Park, it was done on a grand scale. Intended as a quiet retreat for businessmen, the principal funding was supplied by Manchester merchants. The chairman of the Southport Hotel Company, which built it, was a local politician – 'Frontager' Holbrook Gaskell.

The hotel was built at a cost of £60,000 on a 20-acre sea-front site beyond the margin of the built-up area at the end of Weld Road. The 200-foot-long structure contained 75 bedrooms. After it opened in 1866, the extensive grounds were tastefully laid out. At the rear of the hotel there were croquet

Palace Hotel, 1866.

lawns, big enough to accommodate a dozen parties, and a bowling green. These facilities were sheltered from the prevailing south-westerlies by a high embankment, which was topped by the hotel's 650-foot-long promenade, overlooking the shore. In a deep hollow on the inland side of the hotel was an archery field; there was also a playground for children; and the gardens contained walks, bowers and seats. Stables, adjacent to the beach, catered for equestrians. Local residents could buy contracts to use the Palace's outdoor facilities: families were charged 30 shillings a year, and there were concessionary rates for schools. The grounds were also used for special events, such as firework displays, whilst within the hotel magnificent reception rooms housed banquets and concerts. Birkdale Park had acquired a popular social centre of distinction. Nevertheless, despite this local support, the hotel's relative isolation did not augur well for attracting the patronage of residential family visitors, which was essential for commercial success.

HONEYPOT FOR PRIVATE SCHOOLS

Private school promoters quickly followed the builders into the new suburb.

> Private schools spring up when and where they are wanted through private enterprise . . . individuals select such localities . . . as are pleasant and attractive, and where boarders are likely to come. Thus it is that places such as Southport . . . become the happy hunting ground of the private schoolmaster.[24]

43

In the mid-nineteenth century, the majority of middle-class girls were educated in private schools. Running such a school was one of the few career opportunities open to middle-class women, and it presented an option taken by many widows and spinsters. The education given was frequently limited, and there was an emphasis on the acquisition of social graces within a family atmosphere. To establish such a school in rented property required little capital, but the financial rewards were modest. The schools were normally small, and the promoters aimed to attract a choice clientele in order to secure the maximum income. Boarders were preferred to day pupils, as they emphasised the exclusive nature of a school.

Aughton Road's earliest schools appear to have been opened in 1853.[25] It was in that year that Miss M.A. Walsh advertised the opening of a school in 'Hope Cottage', a relatively small dwelling almost opposite York Road. She described the situation as ". . . open, healthy, pleasant and genteel." The fees of £25 per annum for boarders and £4 for day-girls, were very modest. There were extra charges for French, music, and drawing, all important social accomplishments. Although the rent was assessed at only £19 per annum, Miss Walsh also received paying guests, an indication, perhaps, of the difficulty of making a living from such a school. By 1861, she was no longer in residence and 'Hope Cottage' was used for apartments. Also in 1853, Miss Bell opened a similar school in neighbouring 'Birkdale Terrace'. Her fee of £20 emphasised the competitive nature of private schooling. Both schools were at the cheaper end of the market and neither survived long, an indication of the ephemeral nature of many such ventures.

More successful was the school opened by Mrs Elizabeth Belshaw, at 'Enfield Place' in Aughton Road, in 1857. Again her advertisement stressed the health aspects, including the advantages of "salubrious sea air." By 1861, she had nine boarders between the ages of six and fifteen. Girls frequently completed all their schooling in one establishment, although some received part or all of their education from a day or resident governess, in their home.

Boys normally attended a succession of schools. Following early years with a governess or in a dame school close to their home, there was a period in a preparatory school, with a further change at about the age of thirteen. In 1854 the young James Wood, a future Mayor of Southport, following a spell with a Miss Nicholson in Lord Street, "was placed with Mr. Gibson in Aughton Road, an excellent teacher and a good disciplinarian." Although living in Mornington Road, Southport, James was a weekly boarder, spending only the weekends with his family. At the age of twelve he transferred to a boarding school in Sheffield.[26] In 1861, Matthew Gibson employed two resident assistants, including one from France, in his school at 'Willow Bank'. Eight of his eleven boarders were under the age of thirteen, suggesting that his school was mainly, though not exclusively, a preparatory school. Recent construction work at

BIRKDALE PARK: Private Schools 1868

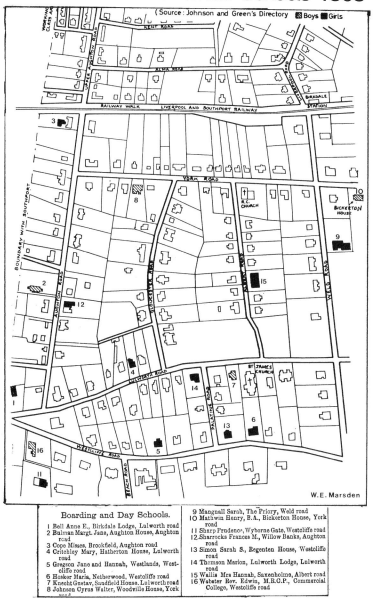

Birkdale: 1868 Street Plan and Private Schools.

'Willow Bank' revealed what appeared to be a schoolboy's cache under the floorboards. This included letters from a Liverpool boarder's parents and an unposted reply, scraps of text books, slate pencils and wrappers, including one from 'Terry's steam-made Lavender Albert Lozenges'.

The conditions in the gracious suburb were those in which private schools thrived. It was perceived as a healthy and select environment; the villas were suitable for use as private schools; the railway was convenient for boarders; whilst the presence of middle-class residents ensured a reservoir of day pupils.

As Birkdale Park developed, successful private school promoters from Southport and wider afield migrated into the new socially secluded suburb. The 1861 census shows eight private schools: seven years later a major national inquiry into secondary education reported that this was one of the north's chief centres for boarding schools.[27] The 1871 census shows that the number of schools had increased to eighteen, with 232 boarders.

Almost two-thirds of the boarders were girls. Typical of the promoters of the girls' schools was Hannah Wallis, a widow, who moved north from Brighton in 1861 and opened a Quaker boarding school – Saxenholme – in Albert Road. A statement in *The Friend* announced that she had:

> . . . taken a house in the healthiest part of this well known and highly esteemed watering place, within a short walking distance of the sea.[28]

The Catholics also opened a denominational school. The Sisters of Notre Dame moved into Weld Road in 1868. The following year they opened a high school for local day-pupils with three girls. The number soon grew, and larger premises had to be acquired.

Boys' schools were less numerous in Birkdale. One of the earliest was a school opened by Cyrus Johnson. In 1853, he advertised Woodville Academy in York Road. It was a modestly-priced school, giving a vocational style of education to prepare boys for business. He was not successful at attracting boarders, and it appears that it was principally a day-school for local boys. Important to all private school promoters were the references they could offer to the parents of intending pupils. The former village schoolmaster was able to use both the Rev. Charles Hesketh, the Rector of North Meols, and the Rev. B. Swift, the Curate of Birkdale, who would have shared the use of the chapel/school on the Common with him. Cyrus was very involved in the community life of Birkdale. He had acted as census enumerator for the township. Having been the secretary for parish committees, he was to be the first clerk to the Birkdale Local Board. His salary for this work and the rent he received for the use of his schoolroom for Board meetings, must have been an important contribution to his budget. Later he several times stood unsuccessfully as a candidate for local office.

Bickerton House School.

More academic schools than Johnson's, specialising in preparing boys for the universities, were frequently run by clergymen. For example, in 1857:

A clergyman long resident in Southport, and now living in Birkdale Park, an Honours man of his university . . . receives five Boarders and six Day Pupils whom his system of instruction will rapidly prepare for a successful College career.[29]

The terms were very expensive – 100 guineas for boarders and 25 guineas for day boys.

The most substantial boys' school was Bickerton House School, founded by Henry Mathwin. He opened a school in Gloucester Road in 1861. During the next decade he moved to a large newly-built school, costing £3,000. It was situated on an extensive site which had been carved out of the undeveloped sand dunes, on the corner of York Road and Oxford Road, at the southern margin of the suburb. By 1871, the school was well established and there were 41 boarders in residence. Mathwin, a staunch Methodist, became an influential religious and civic leader and was a member of the Local Board and the School Board, as well as being a Justice of the Peace. A Liberal, Mathwin was very sensitive to social issues, and campaigned actively for the welfare of the less affluent residents of Birkdale who lived inland of the railway.

St. James' C.E. Church

Landowners attempting to develop residential suburbs frequently sponsored the building of a church, believing that this would help to attract residents. A successful local example is found in the Hesketh Park area of Southport, where the wife of the Rev. Charles Hesketh built All Saints' Church.

In 1850 there was no church in Birkdale, only an afternoon service for the indigenous agricultural residents, which was held in the schoolroom on the distant Common. The Rector appointed the Rev. Benjamin Swift as a curate of the Parish of North Meols, of which Birkdale was part, and gave him ". . . special charge of the Township of Birkdale with the object of preparing it for the erection of a church."[30] The early residents of Birkdale Park lived close to the Southport boundary, and Anglicans amongst them would probably have found Southport's fashionable Christ Church, which offered owned or rented pews for the middle classes in the body of the church and a free gallery for their servants, both more convenient and socially acceptable than a journey to Swift's services on the Common.

Weld-Blundell had appreciated the importance of a church in a residential area and had insisted that Kemp amend his 1848 plan of Birkdale Park to include one. Shortly after his appointment, Swift made an approach to the landowner for help with the site for a church. Weld-Blundell gave a plot in Lulworth Road: thus although not initiating the venture, he did give support. Unlike the school/chapel on the Common, the new church was to be sited in Birkdale Park, ". . . for the convenience of the more respectable parishioners."[31] Nevertheless, it was 1856 before serious efforts were made to raise the necessary money. The Rector, the Rev. Charles Hesketh, opened the fund with a donation of £100, and there was a further £50 from Swift's father-in-law. A bazaar held in the Southport Town Hall raised over £600, but surprisingly the fund was slow to grow. The size of the plot proved to be inadequate for the planned church, and the balance sheet reveals that Weld-Blundell was paid £182 for additional land. The church – St. James' – in red sandstone in the Decorated style, was built beyond the existing houses, although not as far south as proposed on Kemp's plan. Its squat tower, surmounted by a small steeple, rose as an isolated landmark amid a sea of sand dunes. Modest in concept, St. James' cost only £1,900. Nevertheless, there was still a considerable debt when it was opened in 1857, and on the instruction of the Bishop, the consecration was delayed. Further donations included £5 from William Gladstone M.P. and, perhaps surprisingly, ". . . considerable sums were raised in the Manchester area." Affluent Birkdale Park hardly seemed a typical recipient for home mission-type charity. Entries in guide books are normally very congratulatory about churches, but it is very interesting that the *Johnson*

St. James' Church, Lulworth Road.

and Green Guide of 1868 damned St. James' with faint praise, describing it as "... a somewhat antiquated looking building."

Although situated in Birkdale Park, the church served all the Township. Swift was proud of his title – "Vicar of Birkdale". His initial work in Birkdale had been on the Common, and it is claimed that he was particularly successful in getting Park and Common to work together.

Records show that parishioners from throughout Birkdale used the church for weddings and christenings. It seems, however, that Swift was not very successful in attracting a following from amongst the residents of Birkdale Park. After the first few years the "... congregation greatly dwindled", and following a prolonged period of ill health, Swift retired in 1874.[32]

St. Joseph's Roman Catholic Church
The Park also acquired a Catholic church. There were some 2,000 people at the laying of the foundation stone in October 1865. The site, in York Road, was given by Thomas Weld-Blundell, who also gave £1,000 towards the building fund. A staunch Catholic, from an old Catholic family, Thomas Weld-Blundell was a ready and generous benefactor to his own faith. The church was of a light Gothic character, built in brick with stone dressing, and was said to be a good example of the work of the architect Mr. E.W. Pugin (Junior). St. Joseph's, which was opened in May 1867, was not a large church, having accommodation for about 300 people. Given a sound financial start by Weld-Blundell, and having some wealthy parishioners, St. Joseph's experienced little difficulty in raising any necessary funds.

CHAPTER FOUR

BIRKDALE PARK 1874–1912: THE GARDEN SUBURB

... new species of country towns of which Birkdale is one of the best examples ... All that is delightful of the country is preserved – gardens, shrubberies, lawns, with pure air and quietude.

The Progress of Birkdale as a Health Resort, 1882

A BATTLE GROUND FOR COMMERCIAL PRINCES

The Birkdale Park Land Company
By the late 1860s the rate of development in Birkdale Park was slowing down. The street plan published in the 1868 *Johnson and Green Guide* shows that only three new houses had been built to the south of Weld Road. Thomas Weld-Blundell was understandably anxious to develop this wide expanse of virgin sand dunes, and the guide also contains an advertisement, which includes a plan for the second phase of the Birkdale Park Estate, south of Weld Road. Unaware of the existence of the earlier Kemp plan, it is this pictorial plan that Bailey and others have mistakenly assumed was Weld-Blundell's original plan for Birkdale Park. The advertisement informed interested parties that:

> Mr. Lovelady, the steward of T. Weld-Blundell, Esq., attends the Park Hotel every Tuesday between the hours of twelve and four, for the purpose of letting land, or of affording information to intending lessees.

House building continued into Oxford Road, but the pace did not satisfy Weld-Blundell. The Birkdale Park Land Company was the instrument he devised in an attempt to accelerate the development of his Birkdale Park Estate. In 1874 James Richardson, his Liverpool solicitor, formed the Company, which consisted almost exclusively of his own clients and friends. The directors

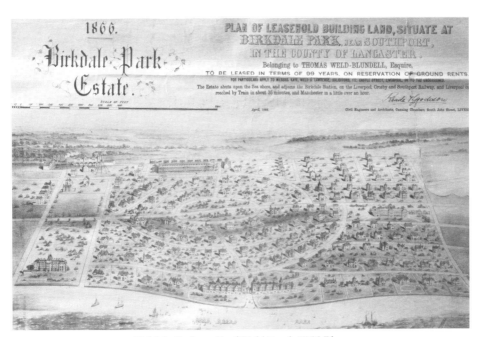

Birkdale Park south of Weld Road: 1866 Plan.

Birkdale Park Land Company Poster, 1874.

thought that the Board needed to include a local personality of some standing. They chose Walter Smith, a building contractor. A Sussex man of modest means, Smith had originally arrived in Southport as a sub-contractor on the Liverpool, Crosby and Southport Railway. He married a local girl, settled in the town and became its principal entrepreneur. Amongst his business interests, he was the promoter and chairman of Southport's massive Winter Gardens, which had been built at a cost of over £90,000. He was also the chairman of the Botanic Gardens Company, and a shareholder in many other local companies. A leading political figure, he had already been Mayor of Southport on three occasions, and was to hold the office again.

With building in Birkdale Park proving sluggish, Weld-Blundell sold 250 acres of sandhills south of Oxford Road to the Birkdale Park Land Company, at a price of £20 an acre. By this device he raised £5,000, without having to wait for the sale of individual plots. Not only would he later be paid ground rent of £6 per acre, but as a director of the new company, he would also receive director's fees and dividends on his holding.

In originally creating Birkdale Park, Thomas Weld-Blundell had personally not been willing to speculate financially and provide "a park", in an attempt to stimulate residential growth. In this second phase, however, he attempted to emulate the successful Southport example of Charles Hesketh, who gave the land for Hesketh Park to the town. The local authority formed the park and paid for a perimeter road, thus opening up Hesketh's previously barren surrounding land for building, and thereby enhancing its value. In 1875, after failing to get the Birkdale Park Land Company to agree to build a park, Weld-Blundell made an offer to the Birkdale Local Board, through that Company, of 50 acres of land for a public park and pleasure ground, to be taken from any part of the Estate between the shore and the railway. Unlike its Southport counterpart, the Birkdale Local Board rejected this scheme, which would have involved it in development and continuing maintenance costs. It was a decision in sympathy with the views of the majority of Birkdale Park residents, who:

> ... did not wish to have a park to attract visitors from the manufacturing towns such as were attracted to Hesketh Park in Southport, but they wished to be quiet and comfortable, and did not want trippers.[1]

Neither did they want an increase in their rates.

For the residents, the 'slacks' between the high sand dunes provided secluded natural pleasure grounds. 'Happy Valley', to the south of the Palace Hotel, was much frequented. In summer, it was:

> ... a broad expanse carpeted with green, dotted with white star flowers, and modest little flowerets of pink and yellow, shut in by a range of miniature mountains.[2]

In hard winters the frozen surface of the slacks provided natural skating rinks. Access to Birkdale's sand hills, including 'Happy Valley', appears to have been restricted from time to time, as it conflicted with the rabbit warren and shooting rights hired out by the estate, and also posed the threat of erosion. When approached by the Birkdale Board on behalf of the residents, both Thomas and Charles Weld-Blundell re-affirmed their commitment to allow access, although this was within defined and sometimes fenced limits.

The Birkdale Park Land Company, with William Penrose as its manager, brought a new urgency to the marketing of Birkdale Park. A permanent office was opened in Weld Road. The agreement between the Estate and the Company allowed it to sell land on 999-year, rather than 99-year leases. Smith soon became the Chairman and the Company prospered, selling 150 acres and paying dividends of 20%. Building continued apace, and in the three years between 1875 and 1878 the rateable value of property in Birkdale rocketed from £24,736 to £44,288. Even with the downturn in trade, which led to the Company selling no land at all in 1879, it still managed a dividend of 15%. Although there was no demand for building plots millions of tons of sand were sold, and transported from the Birkdale hills on a railway laid along the foreshore, to be used to reclaim land enclosed by Southport's new north Promenade. In addition to generating revenue the removal of sand from Birkdale's tall dunes prepared the land for future development. This was a fortuitious coming together of Walter Smith's political interests in Southport with his commercial interests in Birkdale. The downturn in economic fortune was so severe that between 1879 and 1881 the rateable value of property in Birkdale actually fell by almost £2,000. The 1881 census returns show an unusually high number of new houses unoccupied, with some of these properties being looked after by resident caretakers. As the slump continued the Company sustained a trading loss in 1882, and made an immediate call of £1 per share.

The Palace Hotel was also experiencing financial difficulties. Its relatively remote situation was deemed to be one of the reasons for the lack of staying visitors and, in an attempt to facilitate access, the Hotel Company supported a number of schemes. As early as 1871 the Southport Council had asked the Birkdale Board to consider allowing its Promenade to be extended alongside the embankment,(now the site of Rotten Row), to the Palace Hotel. Despite the fact that the hotel was Birkdale's major ratepayer the proposal was rejected, as it was the "avowed wish of the Birkdale Board not to have a Promenade."[3] The Board had no wish to alienate the 'Frontagers' by disturbing their peace and quiet. It was for the same reason that they had rejected a proposal from the Southport Tramways Company to link their line to the Palace Hotel, via Westcliffe Road.

Pressure to extend Southport's Promenade continued, and a clause to this effect was included in the Southport Improvement Bill of 1876. Support from within Birkdale for the Promenade largely came from the Palace Hotel Company and the Birkdale Park Land Company, which offered to defray the cost of building it. Both of these companies stood to gain by improved access to their assets, as did Weld-Blundell, who also supported the Bill. All three also supported Southport's amalgamation proposals, although Weld-Blundell had previously funded the Local Board's opposition to amalgamation at government enquiries! Predictably, opposition to the Promenade came from the Birkdale Local Board, and the 'Frontagers':

> . . . who though they did not buy the land on the foreshore, considered that they had a right to breathe the fine air that came from the Atlantic Ocean, and watch the last rays of the western sun as it dipped into rippling water.[4]

Their opposition was led by George Chamberlain, and they were represented by counsel at the Local Government Board Inquiry. In giving evidence Chamberlain declared that he had chosen to live on Westcliffe Road for "the quiet and seclusion of the neighbourhood."[5] The proposal was rejected. The 'Frontagers' continued to enjoy their private little cliff-top promenades whilst, in the view of their critics, ". . . the poor were prevented from having a Marine Parade."

The Palace Hotel's failure to attract guests in sufficient numbers led to it being forced into liquidation. The Palace Hydropathic and Spa Company was formed to reconstruct the failed hotel as a hydropathic establishment. Interestingly, the chairman of the new company was George Chamberlain and the new hydro was opened in September 1881.

The Southport and Cheshire Lines Extension Railway Company
It was in the financial problems facing the Palace Hotel and the Birkdale Park Land Company that the answer to one of the local riddles lies – the reasons for the arrival of the Southport and Cheshire Lines Extension Railway. The eighteen-mile long Lancashire and Yorkshire Railway Company line linking Southport with Liverpool, had played a major role in the development of Birkdale. The opening of a second line some 30 years later, with a route length of 31 miles, appears to be extraordinary. To think of it as a competing commuter line to Liverpool is, however, to misunderstand the motives of the promoters.

The Lancashire and Yorkshire Railway provided Southport and Birkdale with lines to both Liverpool and Manchester, but both ended at terminus stations. Southport had no direct link with the major national rail networks. A petition supporting such a link attracted signatures from over 2,000 Southport and Birkdale ratepayers. The most obvious route appeared to be through Wigan. Nevertheless, Walter Smith, the Chairman of the Birkdale Park Land Company, successfully urged the adoption of an alternative route, which was some twenty miles longer. He proposed a thirteen-mile long line from Southport to Aintree, the terminus of a circuitous commuter line which the Cheshire Lines Committee had built to serve the southern suburbs of Liverpool. This rambling line did give access to the national network and would allow passengers from Yorkshire and the Midlands to travel to Southport without changing stations in Liverpoool or Manchester. Smith promoted and became chairman of the Southport and Cheshire Lines Extension Railway Company. He was backed by George Chamberlain, the chairman of the Palace Hydropathic and Spa Company, who took £100,000 of the shares, and Weld-Blundell, who bought shares to the value of £1,500 and gave some of the necessary land, thus ensuring that more of his land had to be purchased. This Southport extension, through Altcar and Lydiate, would pass over flat farm land and would be inexpensive to build. Equally important for the promoters, it would have stations by the Birkdale Palace Hotel and behind Southport's Winter Gardens. Critics of this route pointed to the promoters' other commercial involvements, arguing that the line was intended to revive the moribund fortunes of the Winter Gardens Company, the Birkdale Park Land Company, and the Palace Hotel.

This short line was very much a local initiative, and although the prestigious name of the Cheshire Lines Railway was incorporated into the new Company's title, the Cheshire Lines Committee were quick to point out that they had no responsibility, particularly financial, for it. One cynic suggested that the Company was seeking to gain advantage from ". . . wearing borrowed plumes".[6]

The final plan for the railway involved a curve carrying the line from the station by the Palace Hotel away from the embankment across Birkdale beach, before it turned to a Lord Street terminus, alongside the Winter Gardens. This scheme meant the enclosing of a large area of the foreshore. The scheme was opposed by the Local Board and the 'Frontagers'. The railway company was in a relatively weak bargaining position as it needed the support of the Local Board. Consequently it offered to provide Birkdale with a promenade, protected by a substantial sea-wall. Additionally, Weld-Blundell proposed to give the enclosed land to the Township for a 32-acre recreation ground, and the railway company agreed to drain it. The Birkdale Board was pleased with this offer and withdrew its opposition to the necessary Parliamentary Bill. One member declared that they had ". . . received more than they could have expected"; whilst another noted that they had ". . . been treated not only with courtesy, but also generosity."[7]

At the Bill's final Parliamentary stage, the only opposition came from the 'Frontagers'. Not surprisingly, George Chamberlain, previously a strong opponent of even a promenade, was now a vigorous advocate of the railway scheme, for which he was the principal financier. His environmental concern

Birkdale Palace Station and Hotel.

had evaporated and he told the Parliamentary Committee that: "There is a high embankment at the end of my garden and I cannot see what is going on on the foreshore."[8] This, as counsel for the other 'Frontagers' was quick to point out, was a very different song to that which he had sung at the 1876 Parliamentary Enquiry. Several of the 'Frontagers', including Mrs. Ellen Burton of 'The Warren' and her neighbour, Miss Mary Jane Longshaw, gave evidence. They ceded that the length of their gardens and the height of the embankment meant that much of the foreshore could not be seen from their windows. Nevertheless, they insisted that their privacy would be threatened, as the recreation ground would attract hordes of children. Their access to the foreshore through their private tunnels in the embankment would be reduced, and their property would be threatened by vibration. Another 'Frontager', Mr. Percival, an amateur cultivator of orchids living at 'Clevelands', feared that his plants would be damaged by the smoke.

Much discussion centred on the "dismal swamp". The pools in front of Rotten Row, in which young boys fished, were full of noisy "frogs of a peculiar species – neither frogs nor toads" – presumably natterjacks, (now a relatively rare species which still survive in their protected duneland habitat, and have long been known as the "Birkdale Nightingales"). Supporters of the railway claimed that the lagoons were a nuisance and a threat to health, whilst the 'Frontagers' now adopted a more environmentally friendly view of them. To one side the nightly croaking of the natterjacks was a pleasant country song, whilst to the other it was an unbearable cacophony. Although the 'Frontagers'

56

opposition was not sufficient to defeat the Bill, the House of Lords' Committee did, at this late stage, insert some important new clauses. One of these which was to assume great importance in the future was the ruling that the Company should be responsible for the "forming and maintenance in good order" of the recreation ground.[9]

As Walter Smith was to be the contractor building the line, he had resigned as chairman of the railway company and been replaced by Weld-Blundell. Bad weather contributed to delays in construction and the project fell behind schedule. The necessity for a sea-wall to protect the railway was soon demonstrated. In 1883, the coincidence of winter storms and high tides led to a breach in the wall and extensive damage to the railway works. Smith's problems were not confined to construction work. Relationships with his commercial collaborators appear to have deteriorated. He was replaced as chairman of the Birkdale Park Land Company by David Ratcliffe of Formby Hall, who was also Weld-Blundell's deputy chairman in the railway company. His relationship with the Land Company had soured to such an extent that it took legal action to recover £12.10s, which, it was claimed, Smith had pocketed from the sale of sand for the Southport Promenade reclamation. In building the railway, Smith ran into financial difficulties. At a Company meeting, with construction eleven months behind schedule, the chairman told the shareholders that: "The contractor had entered into the contract knowing full well what he had to do."[10] He had agreed a fixed price and there were to be no additional payments to compensate him for his problems. Unfortunately, Smith had committed all his available capital to the project, and had accepted payment from the Company in the form of shares. His creditors were pressing him and he was unable to convert his only major assets – shares in the railway company – into cash. He suffered a stroke and, following brief proceedings, was declared bankrupt.

The Southport and Cheshire Lines Extension Railway, on which Smith pinned so many hopes, was not to be his commercial salvation. Nevertheless, there is still much tangible evidence of his impact on the local community. In addition to his commercial work, his political involvement included the boulevard scheme on Lord Street, the re-building and northern extension of Southport's Promenade, and the building of the Cambridge Hall. Bankruptcy led to the loss of his Southport aldermanic seat. Friends had to rally round to prevent the sale of silver presentation sets given to him by the Southport Corporation, and a public subscription provided some £1,200 for an annuity. It would be nice to think that in his remaining years, at 44 Aughton Road, he could have quietly played bowls at the nearby Aughton Road Birkdale Club, which he founded. This was not to be. Paralysis confined him to a wheelchair and he died in 1887.

In an attempt to raise revenue the line, although not completely finished, was officially opened on 1st September 1884. The railway's scenic approach through the dunes and across the beach caused a commentator to judge that: "A better route . . . for conveying a good first impression of Southport could not be devised."[11] The same spectacular approach is now enjoyed by motorists on the Coast Road, which is built on the track of the railway. It was commercial results, however, rather than aesthetic approval that shareholders sought. Birkdale Palace Station did not open until the summer of 1885. On the August Bank holiday, it was estimated that 12,000 people had arrived at Southport's Lord Street Station. Nevertheless, traffic on the line was slow to build up, the circuitous approach apparently deterring excursionists. When no dividends were forthcoming the shareholders were quick to express their dissatisfaction with the directors. At the annual meeting in 1886, the charge was repeated that the Winter Gardens, the Birkdale Park Land Company and the Palace Hotel had benefited, whilst the interests of the shareholders had been ignored. Attacks were made on the Chairman, Thomas Weld-Blundell, and his deputy, David Ratcliffe. Both were frequent absentees from meetings: the former was resident in the south, whilst the latter was prevented from attending by civic duties in Liverpool. A critic asked why these minor shareholders – it appears that they now held only 200 shares each – should exercise so much power. Both were replaced as directors. It seems that their involvement with the railway had cost them little and served their commercial ends well, a stark contrast to the fate of Walter Smith.

Although there was a modest improvement in the amount of traffic carried, the net revenue stayed stubbornly below the figure needed to service the charges on money the Company had had to raise, and no dividends were paid. This small local company was faced with an increasing deficit, whilst legal obligations prevented it from cutting its losses and closing down the line. The Company was saved from further disaster by coming to an arrangement with the Cheshire Lines Committee, which was run by a consortium of major national railway companies. A new Parliamentary Bill was presented in 1889 and the Committee took over the running of the line. There were still no dividends for the unfortunate shareholders of the local company, but at least they had been saved from even worse troubles.

THE SPOILS OF WAR

The Esplanade
Despite the railway company's financial problems, the Birkdale Local Board insisted on receiving its rights under the 1882 Act. The Company had agreed to provide a promenade between the Palace Hotel and the Royal Hotel, on Southport's Promenade. It became known as the Esplanade and can still be seen, being the approach road to the Caravan Club site. It consisted of a broad

carriage-way and tiled pavement. Throughout the construction the Board complained about the poor quality of the surface. Members alleged that the asphalt was mixed with sand and could easily be kicked up, and the Board insisted that the carriage-way be remade. Prevarication continued, but the Company opened the Esplanade to the public and it proved to be very popular. The Board was still not satisfied with the surface, and repeatedly refused to take possession. Meanwhile the prevailing winds piled sand on to the road and made the carriage-way almost unusable. Neither party would accept responsibility to clear the sand, and the drifts threatened to engulf it completely. In 1886, following yet further re-surfacing, the Esplanade was eventually adopted.

In the absence of regular attention, the road was soon covered once again by thousands of tons of sand. This was cleared on the occasion of the Prince of Wales' visit to inspect the Hussars on the beach, but normally the Birkdale authority was not prepared to spend money for this purpose. They did offer sand free of cost to builders and although up to 60 tons a week was removed, the problem remained. The neglect extended to the carriage-way, which was studded with depressions and ruts, whilst the attractive twisted iron railings on the sea wall went unpainted and soon rusted. All this was in sharp contrast to the Southport length, which had been widened and linked to the new Marine Drive. In truth, Birkdale didn't want a popular Esplanade and the trippers it might attract. The *Southport Visiter* accurately summarised the position:

> Having hardly the same ambitions and objects as our watering place population, the Birkdale people have not concerned themselves much about this. If the Esplanade had been used by them the District Council would have taken the matter firmly in hand years ago.[12]

Significantly, there was no photograph of the Esplanade in the Council's lavishly illustrated *Guide Book*.

Victoria Park
Relationships between the Birkdale Local Board and the Railway Company had become very fraught, as the Board sought to ensure that all the detailed provisions of the 1882 Act relating to the recreation ground were met, while the Company attempted to restrict its liability to the drainage and grassing of the site – in the style of 'The Stray', at Harrogate. The House of Lords' Committee had nominated Mr. Elias Dorning of Manchester to prepare a plan for the lay-out of the recreation ground. Drainage ditches had to be dug, the lagoons filled and thousands of tons of new top-soil brought in before the planting programme could be undertaken, and the park was not ready, as promised, when the railway was opened in 1884. The Railway Company put in over 30,000 trees, shrubs and plants. This satisfied Mr. Dorning that it had

completed its work, according to his specifications, and the Company was prepared to hand the park over to the Board in 1887. The Board claimed, however, that according to the 1882 Act, the Company was under an obligation not only to form the gardens, but also to maintain them in perpetuity. This was its interpretation of the ambiguously worded clause which had been inserted after the 'Frontagers' last stand. The Company claimed that its responsibility for maintenance was restricted to the drainage; the Board claimed it was total maintenance. Both sides took legal advice and although the Company had passed over the keys to the Board, the park gates remained locked. The iron railings rusted, whilst plants died, being choked by weeds and blasted by wind, sand and salt-spray. The case went to the Court of Appeal and the Board's interpretation of the hastily drawn-up clause was upheld. The Company estimated that it had already spent over £20,000 providing Birkdale with the Esplanade and park. While the wrangling continued the Company opened the park to the public in 1890: once again a major Birkdale event which passed without ceremony or celebration. Finally, two years later, the Board agreed to a settlement of £1,000 in return for accepting responsibility for maintenance, and the park passed into its hands. Not surprisingly, the shareholders of the ailing railway company were told that it had been ". . . put to very great expense in many ways by the local authorities of Birkdale".[13]

Birkdale's park adjoined a much smaller park across the Southport boundary, which its neighbour had quickly laid out with ornamental gardens, a lake, bowling greens and pitches for other games. The Southport Recreation Ground had been opened with much civic pomp as part of the Queen's Jubilee celebrations in 1887. The two parks now form Victoria Park, but characteristically Birkdale sealed the boundary between them with a hedge, shrubberies and railings – a veritable iron curtain.

Birkdale's park was known as Birkdale Recreation Ground, and it was belatedly christened Victoria Park in 1898. For many years the only recreation available in the park was to walk on the asphalt paths, and not surprisingly the park was little used. The Council had obtained a large and profitable hayfield, yielding two crops a year! At first it insisted that the grass needed time to settle, before the surface was fit for the playing of games. This explanation was wearing a little thin after ten years.

The Council did begin to develop a portion of the park at the south end, distant from Southport. There was an avenue of well tended gardens, linking Beach Road to a footbridge over the railway. In 1897, 60 ornamental trees were donated and planted along this avenue to commemorate the Queen's Jubilee, and it was later known as Jubilee Avenue. It became a custom for every Birkdale councillor to plant a tree there. Most of the £1,000 received from the railway company was spent on two shelters for this area. In 1900 a lodge was also erected. Following an occasion when a couple were summonsed for

Victoria Park – playing fields and haystacks, 1901.

Victoria Park. Birkdale

Victoria Park – lodge and Jubilee Avenue.

"misconducting" themselves in one of the shelters, the uniformed park-keeper, Mr. Holden, was given the rank of special constable.

The development of the park (or relative lack of it) was much influenced by the lobby of powerful ratepayers of Birkdale Park, particularly the 'Frontagers'. They feared that an attractive landscaped park could develop like the Marine Park in Southport, with hordes of trippers. When swings were installed, Henry Taylor, an eminent local antiquarian, acted as spokesman for the 'Frontagers' and presented their memorial of objection to the Council:

> Whenever they retired to take a stroll in their private grounds they were bound to witness sights which were disgusting, and hear language which was not fit for a Christian. Undesirable visitors of both sexes lounged and swung in improper attitudes.[14]

The Council decided to remove the ropes and seats from the swings. These were reinstated only when the park was to be used by Birkdale children on supervised occasions such as Sunday School outings. The park, on the westward fringe of the township, was clearly in the wrong place to be used regularly by the children from the densely populated area of East Birkdale. Mr. Holden, the keeper, ensured that it was not a fun area:

> When a child steps on the grass it leads to loud shouting and whistling from the over-officious gentleman in charge, who doubtless imagines his sole duty is to terrify children as much as possible.[15]

Another contributing factor to the Council's reluctance to develop sports pitches was the fact that, because of conditions in the Act, it was not legally permitted to charge for their use. Eventually it did develop some pitches, and derived an income by charging for their preparation and for the use of nets and other apparatus. It quickly realised that the park could become an income-generating asset. Nevertheless, the park was not widely used by the people of Birkdale and became principally a playing field for girls from Birkdale Park's many private schools. The emphasis was on the gentler sports, particularly tennis, hockey and croquet, and pitches for these games were located to the south of Jubilee Avenue.

There was a limited number of pitches for rugby, football and cricket on the wide open spaces to the north of the avenue. Even so, in 1900 over two-thirds of the park were still devoted to growing hay. Haymaking required the employment of twelve men and three teams of horses, and the stacks, which were insured by the Board, were a feature of the landscape. Birkdale Rugby Club, later replaced by Southport Olympic, played regularly on the park. Football clubs, which paid £5 a year for a pitch, seemed to find the conditions less to their liking and did not stay long. The ground was even less suitable for cricket, with only a narrow strip being cut for the wicket, whilst the rest of the grass was left long.

To hit only along the ground, however hard, was only rewarded by a single. However, knock the ball thirty yards away in the air would lead to a game of hide-and-seek with fielders looking for the ball in thick undergrowth.[16]

The Council was still selling hay in 1907. By 1912, it had 25 tenants: the rugby club and one football club (ironically it was a Southport club, Hesketh Park F.C., there being no sports facilities in that landscaped park), hockey (the six tenants were mainly schools), cricket (the two clubs, West End and St. Paul's, are still playing in the Southport and District League), tennis (the twelve tenants included The Park Club), bowls, and croquet.

Southport consistently pressed to have the fence between the two parks opened. Birkdale resisted, believing that to do so would lead to a considerable increase in what it termed "nuisance". Southport offered to build double gates with Birkdale holding the key, but all to no avail. When amalgamation was nearing, the members of the Park Committee, mindful that they might soon be councillors of greater Southport, agreed to consider this question yet again. Even at this late stage, however, they resolved to keep the two parks separate:

Any willingness to accede had to give way to pressure from prominent ratepayers, who do not look with favour on the amalgamation of the two parks.[17]

The 'Frontagers' truly cast a long shadow.

Rotten Row

Rotten Row, the space between the foot of the embankment and Victoria Park, had been left as a sandy strip. Shrubs and trees planted along the margin of the park had made it into a more sheltered way and it continued to enjoy its popularity with the Township's equestrians. It was convenient to the riding stables in Aughton and Weld Roads. In fact riding masters had to be banned from using it for training horses, circling on long lunge reins.

The Southport and Cheshire Lines Extension Company Act had included a clause requiring the Company to construct a 36-foot wide road the length of Rotten Row. It had suited Birkdale not to insist on this being done. Part of Rotten Row was, however, in Southport and in 1905, under pressure from its neighbour, Birkdale agreed to join in an approach to the Company. To the chagrin of its shareholders, the impoverished Company paid £700 for release from any further liability for the road. Southport quickly used its share to surface its length of Rotten Row. Birkdale re-curbed and channelled the roadway, but did not surface it. To do so would have been to extend Southport's Promenade to the Palace Hotel, a development that the Birkdale authority had long resisted. Southport accused Birkdale of failing to use the money for the purpose laid down in the Act. Eventually, Birkdale agreed to asphalt the surface from the Southport boundary as far as the park lodge, and cover the remainder with loose cinders, for the benefit of the equestrians. This solution had the merit of "surfacing" all of Rotten Row, without providing a through way for carriages. As with the Esplanade, there was no photograph of Rotten Row in the township guide. In yet another display of their economic power the 'Frontagers' sent a petition to the Council objecting to an unsightly line of overhead telephone cables on posts down Rotten Row. The telephone company replaced them with underground cables.

Birkdale had exacted a heavy price from the Southport and Cheshire Lines Extension Railway Company. It seems a cruel irony that Birkdale Park's fear of trippers meant that these sea-front 'spoils of war' were not really wanted.

BIRKDALE PARK: CASTLES IN THE SAND

Within seven years of the formation of the Birkdale Park Land Company, over 50 villas had been built along Lancaster, Waterloo and Trafalgar Roads up to, and just beyond, Grosvenor Road. Despite periodic economic depressions, which adversely affected the housing market, the Company set its mind against dilution and the building of cheaper houses. The area shows none of the social ambiguity which characterised the early development of Birkdale Park, north of Weld Road. Phase Two of Birkdale Park, south of Weld Road, was a consistently high-class residential suburb. These expensive villas, hard by the dunes at the southern edge of the built-up area, were truly "Castles in the Sand". The nearest approach to compromise appears to have occurred in Regent Road when, in 1889, neighbours objected to the erection of what they described as "a row of cottages" rather than one respectable detached house. A developer had placed two houses on a single plot and in doing so had approached the margins of the site. Although cramped these houses were hardly cottages, being worth about £1,200. Nevertheless, the Land Company sympathised with the complaints and agreed to refuse anything of this description in the future.

The number of resident servants present in these villas was a firm indication of the superior nature of this affluent suburb. In 1881, all the new houses south of Weld Road had servants, and there were only eleven out of the 49 with a single servant, whilst the same number had three or more. Ten years later 33 out of the 135 houses had only a single servant, whilst 43 had three or more. Life below stairs was hard and rewards were small. Advertisements showed that general servants earned less than £20 per annum. A good "character" was essential for those seeking employment as servants. Such was the demand for servants in Birkdale Park that the 'Alexandra Agency' was opened in Liverpool Road to provide: "Superior servants with good testimonials". Those servants

'Belair', Trafalgar Road.

who did err were severely punished. In 1889, three "previously respectable young women" stole what were described as trifles from their employer in Regent Road. Although this was their first offence, they were sentenced to six, four, and three months hard labour. One of the largest establishments was at 'Lismore', the Waterloo Road home of sugar refiner William Macfie, the commander of the Volunteers, and a leading local politician. He lived there with his wife and six children. In 1891 they were looked after by eight resident servants, including a page.

In 1888 a commentator in the *Liverpool Porcupine* noted the number of "Liverpool merchant princes" resident in Birkdale: "In addition to the stopping trains there are two expresses which leave, filled mostly with first class passengers."[18] In 1900 the same newspaper suggested that Birkdale Park was ". . . much favoured by the legal profession of Liverpool." There were so many commuters using Birkdale Station that it justified the opening of a bookstall. In 1904 this link to Liverpool was improved when the Company electrified it, using a three-rail system, at a cost of £400,000. It was said that this was the first line in England to be so developed, and the Company claimed that expresses could complete the journey to Liverpool in twenty minutes. A journey time of 50 minutes was the fastest claimed by its Cheshire Lines rival. Although many residents of the Park were living on independent incomes, the vast majority of those who were in employment worked elsewhere. This was in marked contrast to the residents of Southport, the bulk of whom made their living in

Birkdale Station staff.

Electric Train at Ainsdale, c. 1910.

the town. This fact goes a long way to explain the different attitudes of the two communities to visitors and solitude.

In addition to the trains from the two stations, the residents of the Park were well provided with other forms of transport which facilitated their access to churches, shops, and entertainments in Southport. Although much of Birkdale Park was not served by the tramway there was also an omnibus service. In addition to privately-owned carriages, the Local Board licensed over 50 – landaus, victorias and broughams. These carriages plied for hire from designated cabstands. There were frequent campaigns for these to have shelters for the cabbies. The problem came when there was not the space for them to go on an island in the middle of the road. Residents wished to have cabs available, but no one wanted the stands immediately outside their property.

When the first motor taxi was licensed in Birkdale in 1909 it was not allowed a stand, and had to ply for hire from its garage. Predictably, private motor cars were quickly popular in Birkdale. Several car dealers set up business in the township and the Council issued licences to petrol retailers. Although there was an unusually high number of cars in Birkdale, not all the residents favoured their introduction. The Minutes of the Highway Committee contain letters of complaint about cars being driven at excessive speeds. Notice boards cautioning motorists to drive slowly were erected in the township, and the

Tram in York Road.

Committee also wrote to the magistrates and the police, who subsequently conducted a purge against speedy and reckless drivers. Motorists were not to disturb the tranquillity of Birkdale Park. Nevertheless, motoring proved to be irresistible to many of the Park's affluent residents. In 1905 the Health, Cemetery and Plans Committee approved J. Mather's plan to build a "motor shed" at his Lancaster Road home; Mr. Hassall, of 24 Waterloo Road, paid £570 for his 20 horse-power Beeston Humber Landaulette, to seat six; whilst Kate Ryley, of Regent Road, took delivery of a car in 1905 and immediately drove it on an excursion to Lancaster. She later used it to transport members of the Lancashire Education Committee on visits to schools, and to take crippled children on outings. Perhaps the most romantic tale of a Birkdale motorist involved the "handsome, laughing" Lieutenant Gerald Klombies of 14 Albert Road:

> Having a magnificent motor, he was a frequent visitor to London from his regiment (Queens Bays) at Hounslow. Going to the Gaiety Theatre he at once fell in love with Miss Adelina Baffe – appearing as Lolita, one of the cigarette girls in "Havanna". They were married at Holborn Registry Office before the Saturday matinee, followed by a dinner party at the Waldorf Hotel.[19]

Even before Birkdale belatedly obtained its park, the area had firmly established its reputation as a garden suburb. A letter to the editor of the *Southport Visiter* in 1888 spoke of:

> . . . tasteful gardens, which, with carefully tended lawns, beautiful trees, with their graceful foliage and refreshingly welcome shade, and the glorious display of exquisite flowers, with every exquisite variation of form, hues and odours, show that a great love of beauty exists in the minds of those who dwell in this favoured region.[20]

It also demonstrated the wealth of the inhabitants who could afford to import the topsoil and manure necessary to render the sand fertiie, and to pay to employ Birkdale's legion of gardeners. Fairbridge and Hatch tipped 200 loads of "sludge" on the gardens of new houses they built in Lancaster Road. Although a second nursery was opened by William Smith, at 31 Aughton Road, it is probable that the majority of the trees and shrubs came from Birkdale's principal nurseryman, George Davies, who also advised the Council on the planting of Victoria Park. Anyone who has tried to cultivate Birkdale sand will know how little body it has and the speed with which it dries out. Mrs Sawyer, the proprietrix of the Park Hotel, held the patent for several portable sprinkling machines. The placing of full-page illustrated advertisements in the local directories marks her as an enterprising business woman.

One of the first houses to be built in Birkdale Park was 'Birkdale Lodge' in Lulworth Road. It was sold in 1914, following the death of the owner. A detailed illustrated catalogue for the sale of the house and its contents has survived and helps to build a picture of life in one of the Park's villas, which still stands in very much its original form.

Robert Mather was a Bolton-born wine merchant with a business in Chapel Street, Southport. Aged 73 when he died, he had lived in 'Birkdale Lodge' since 1872 and raised his family there. He appears to have had sporting interests, particularly in coursing and horse-racing. The house contained models and engravings of champions and presentation cups, whilst the library included many volumes of stud books. The presence of a pair of woods and a jack suggests that he played bowls. There was also a croquet set for use on the lawn. The house contained a billiard room with a full-size table. A mahogany rack containing 20 cues indicates that this was a popular facility. The billiard room was decorated with a valuable set of 40 framed signed proof etchings by W. Dendy Sadler.

Leisure was important to the middle classes, and the furniture included a card table. It appears that the bridge-playing craze hit Birkdale early in the twentieth century. Mrs. Stephenson, the wife of a former vicar, alleged that bridge parties were very prevalent, giving Birkdale ". . . a Mayfair of its own."[21] Mather had two daughters, and piano playing was a desirable social accomplishment for middle-class girls. The family had an upright grand piano and a further piano with a self-playing attachment, a gramophone, and a large twelve-tune music box. The library was modest in size, containing some 400 undistinguished volumes. There was an extensive collection of paintings in the house, including three watercolours of a cottage in Ainsdale, painted by different artists in 1875. There was a further watercolour of the Ainsdale windmill. There were engravings of several politicians, from both major parties, and an autographed photograph of Gladstone. Interestingly there was also a portrait of the landowner – Charles Weld-Blundell. These pictures were hung in a magnificent large central oak-panelled hall, which rose to the full height of the house. The hall dominated the house, and the oak fire-place and balustrades were heavily carved. There was a stained-glass window on the stairway, which led to a galleried landing. To summon the family to meals there was a large "sonorous gong".

In the dining room the oak table, with ebony inlay, was five feet wide and ten inserting leaves could extend it to almost 24 feet. The dinner service was for eighteen diners. The drawing room was the principal entertaining room and contained many of the house's finest ornaments, paintings and pieces of furniture, including some by Sheraton. The furnishings of the morning room underline its functions. Here were to be found everyday items such as: newspaper rack, thermometer, barometer, writing desk, stationery, and rocking chairs. There was also a mahogany dining-suite. The drawing room, dining room, morning room, billiard room and library were all approached by doors

'Birkdale Lodge' – dining room.

leading from the central hall. A further door gave access to a well-stocked iron-framed conservatory; the garden also contained a fernery, vinery and peach house.

The three-stalled stable housed a well-matched pair of carriage horses, and in the coach-house there were four rubber tyred carriages. These were a victoria, a brougham, a landau, and a six-seater phaeton wagonette. All the carriages were painted red, dark green and black.

In 1891 the establishment consisted of three resident servants: a 24-year-old waitress from Liverpool, a 19-year-old Welsh housemaid, and a 24-year-old cook from Manchester. The three maids' bedrooms were situated over the kitchen and scullery and were approached by the back stairs. Access to the servants' quarters was by a discreet side entrance. In the yard was a wash-house.

There were two galvanised washing tubs, but at the heart of the wash, the dolly-tub was of oak. The wringing machine was locally made by "Hodge of Southport."

'Birkdale Lodge' was not one of Birkdale Park's great mansions, on the scale of 'Clairville' or 'The Warren', nevertheless it was probably typical of many of the villas, and like many others it had also served as a private school. Cyrus Johnson had transferred there from York Road. Unfortunately he enjoyed little success and the building of the Birkdale Town Hall meant a loss of income as the Board ceased to use his premises for meetings. No longer the Clerk to the Board, he was summonsed for non-payment of rates and moved to more modest premises in Belmont Street.

BIRKDALE PARK: A HAVEN FOR INVALIDS AND THE RETIRED

From its inception, Birkdale Park had been popular with both men and women living from unearned income. Although more Liverpool businessmen were settling in the township, there were still approximately 120 out of the 260 heads of household in this category in 1881, and just over two-thirds of them were women. Birkdale Park had been marketed as a health resort. In 1882 *The Progress of Birkdale as a Health Resort* was published. It spoke of the Park, with its quiet asphalt roads, offering ". . . calm and life restoring quietude". Anything which disturbed this middle-class suburban tranquillity attracted fierce criticism. There were regular complaints about "The Game of Knockemdown" – the toppling of coping stones off walls, and caps off gate pillars. Even the penalty of a £5 fine or four months imprisonment did not appear to deter the nineteenth century vandals. On one occasion the Chairman of the Bench noted the irony when the culprit turned out to be a bricklayer. There were also frequent reports and complaints about begging. Another cause of irritation was the seats that the Council bought to place on the pavements. Ratepayers objected to having them placed outside their homes, as they led to ". . . annoyance of a serious nature caused by lovers in the evening hours."[22]

The township had appointed a Medical Officer in 1873, and he regularly reported on the health-giving "ozone level" in Birkdale. There were occasions when there were claims and counter-claims as to whether the level was better than that in Southport. Birkdale's neighbour did have the advantage of taking its readings at the hilltop station in Hesketh Park. Birkdale Park enjoyed much superior public cleansing arrangements to those obtaining in Southport. Bins were introduced for the disposal of domestic refuse in 1901. They were emptied twice a week. Unlike the ashpits they superseded, emptying was done by day, rather than at night. This new service cost householders 10s 6d a year and was adopted by a large majority of the Park's residents, while Southport, like the rest of Birkdale, persisted with ashpits.

Adding to its reputation as a health resort Birkdale had two major hydropathic institutions. The promoters of the Smedley Hydro recognised the potential afforded by this residential suburb, with its reputation as a healthy locality. The hydropathic facilities were based on the system employed by the late Mr. Smedley of Matlock, and the new hotel adopted his name. Unlike the Palace Hotel, opening the Smedley in 1877 had involved no massive outlay of

Smedley Hydropathic Hotel.

Smedley Hydropathic Hotel – ballroom.

capital. The building in Trafalgar Road had been intended for use as a college. Early success meant that a wing was quickly added. By 1879 the Company reported that the ". . . number of guests had exceeded their most sanguine anticipation."[23] This claim appears to have had some substance, as a second new wing was built.

The medical director was Dr. Barnardo. Interestingly there was also a branch of his illustrious brother's residential homes for young cripples in Trafalgar Road. In addition to the treatment rooms, the Smedley offered drawing rooms, reading and writing rooms, billiard and smoking rooms. In the grounds there were conservatories and ornamental gardens, as well as tennis courts and a croquet green. Thomas Weld-Blundell's detachment from the day-to-day running of the Estate was demonstrated when he was driving past the Smedley during one of his occasional visits to Birkdale, and had to ask his driver what place it was.

The Company had found a niche in the market and regularly paid a dividend of up to 6%, whilst continuing to spend on upgrading facilities. A congratulatory account of the hotel, in the *Christian Herald*, suggested that "Cupid seems very busy in this house and many a son-in-law has been found there."[24]

The success of the Smedley probably influenced the reconstruction of the failed Palace Hotel as a hydropathic establishment. Part of the financial re-organisation of the new Company involved selling off land in front of the hotel for house building. The area of the plot was reduced to five acres – a quarter of its original size – and much of the pleasure gardens was lost. The building underwent extensive renovation and a variety of baths was installed, including a plunge. The hydro was based on a system which had been recently introduced in Buxton's newest hotel. The Company had a pipe built to draw salt water from the sea. Another feature was the inhaling room. To facilitate access, an elevator to all floors was installed. The new hydro was opened in September 1881, with Dr. Henry Blumberg as medical director, and a resident staff of over 60. The hotel later installed the first electric lighting system in Birkdale, with its own steam-driven generator.

The hydro's target clientele was the really wealthy. F.H. Cheetham, a contemporary local historian, judged that ". . . much as it was appreciated by 'the few', 'the many' did not patronise it."[25] By 1910 the Palace Hotel was again in financial trouble and for sale.

There were no doctors resident in Birkdale in 1868, but by 1881 there were six, and by 1911 the number had grown to nineteen. York Road became the focus for medical and dental practitioners, thus helping to lift this road's social image. In 1881 there were two doctors living in York Road, including Dr. Cooper Harrison who ran a residential Spinal Institute at number 29. The 1891 census shows five doctors in the road; while by 1911 there were six doctors along with four dentists in practice. York Road's medical establishment was completed by a pharmacy. In ministering to the residents of the Park, the doctors were supported by nurses supplied by "Birkdale Trained Nurses", whose regulations included the requirement that:

> No wines, spirits or malt liquors should be given to the nurses, unless ordered by the doctor, but when on night duty extra tea, coffee or cocoa, together with food should be provided.[26]

A further facility for invalids was Birkdale's half dozen licensed bathchairmen, who plied for hire from outside the Town Hall and the hotels. George Kilvert, the lard manufacturer, was a relatively sickly man, who was typical of many who came to settle in Birkdale: "A need for a health trip was the means of his introduction to Birkdale and he found the place suited to himself."[27] When Thomas Weld-Blundell's widow Teresa was terminally ill, in 1887, she accepted medical advice and moved to a house in Birkdale – 17 Lulworth Road.

PRIVATE SCHOOLS: AN EXTRAORDINARY COTTAGE INDUSTRY

Mrs. Kitchener, an Assistant Commissioner for the 1895 Royal Commission on Secondary Education, was staggered by the number of private schools she discovered during a walk around Birkdale Park. She reported that it teemed with them, ". . . there being more brass plates than one could count." The Park had become a centre for girls' 'finishing schools', the socially select garden suburb being particularly attractive to boarders. Girls constituted almost three-quarters of all pupils, and of the 303 girls boarding, in 1881, almost two-thirds were over the age of fourteen, a clear indication of the emergence of specialist 'finishing schools'. Unlike the early ventures on the fringe of the Park, these schools, which were mainly located south of Weld Road, tended to be expensive, substantial, and relatively permanent. Also, in the view of Mrs. Kitchener, "Health and all that appertains to it" was certainly a critical consideration for the parents of potential boarders.

A three-page prospectus has survived for one such school – Leighton College, in Lulworth Road. Miss A. Batham, who conducted the school with her two spinster sisters and a resident assistant, had previously run a smaller school in Southport. The prospectus claims that:

> Birkdale is acknowledged to be the healthiest suburb of Southport, and Leighton College is pleasantly situated at a very short distance from the shore.

The proximity of stations on two different railway lines is also noted. The premises of Leighton College demonstrate the scale, style and spacious setting

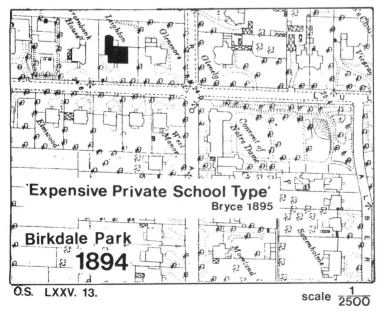

Leighton College.

of the Birkdale Park villas and their suitability for use as boarding schools. The prospectus describes the building as:

> . . . especially adapted for school purposes . . . The Dining Room and the Recreation Hall are 50ft. long and 24ft. wide, the former being 14ft. high.

The promoters attempted to allay parental concern about physical conditions by declaring that ". . . during the cold season (the premises) are kept at a judicious temperature throughout by mean of hot water pipes." The basic fee for boarders was up to 65 guineas per annum, whilst charges for day boarders were up to 32 guineas. There was also a range of chargeable extras including the teaching of languages, music, singing, painting and drawing. As was common in Birkdale Park, the Principal required a term's notice prior to the removal of a pupil. This device afforded protection against capricious withdrawal and loss of income. The Misses Batham claimed unspecified success in preparing girls for external examinations. They did, however, specify the names and addresses of 26 worthy referees whom parents of prospective pupils were permitted to approach, in relation to the promoters' intentions to:

> surround their pupils with the comforts of home and make it their earnest endeavour to combine moral and religious training with intellectual culture.

Another 'finishing'-type school was Malvern House, in Waterloo Road. Miss Hobbs, an example of the upward mobility of Birkdale's educational entrepreneurs, had earlier run a school in Aughton Road. By the end of the century, Malvern House had about 60 pupils, of whom half were boarders. The majority of the day pupils lived in Birkdale Park. Mrs. Simon, yet another migrant from Aughton Road, was successful with her Wintersdorf School, in Trafalgar Road. Approximately 30 of the 80 pupils were local day girls.

Saxenholme, opened by Hannah Wallis, had prospered and in 1876 she moved to a larger and more commodious house – Brighthelmston – she had built in Waterloo Road. There were 48 boarders in residence at the time of the 1881 census. The average age of these girls was over fourteen, confirming that this was indeed a 'finishing school'. There were also about two dozen day girls, who paid fees of between nine and 21 guineas per annum. The Local Examination results appeared to be the best for a girls' school in Birkdale. Saxenholme was successfully continued by the Misses Horner and, like Brighthelmston, it was attended by generations of residents of the Park and survived until comparatively recently.

A feature of Birkdale's girls' schools was the attention given to games. Mrs. Kitchener noted that games:

Much of this aspect was probably influenced by Mr. A. Alexander, a physical education specialist of national significance, who opened his Southport Physical Training College in York Road in 1891. The College, which he ran with his wife and a number of assistants, was established to prepare female students "to take entire charge of the indoor and outdoor games of pupils, and to foster all that is healthy in the school."[28] His students were successful in gaining posts in girls' schools throughout the kingdom. One of the factors which attracted him to Birkdale was the number of girls' schools which allowed practice facilities for the students during their two-year course. The prospectus shows the College to be well equipped; while games, which required more space than was available on the court behind the College, were played on Victoria Park. Success led to expansion, and by 1911 it occupied numbers 8 and 9 in York Road and number 40 in adjoining Aughton Road.

Although much fewer in number than those for girls, there were also boys' schools in Birkdale Park. The most substantial was Bickerton House. From the early 1880s, Henry Mathwin's son, a Cambridge mathematics graduate, took over its running. Three of the six assistant teachers were graduates, and pupils distinguished themselves in the University Local Examinations. At the 1871 Census Bickerton House had as many as 41 boarders. In the closing decades of the century, it became more important as a local day school, day boys comprising over 80% of the pupils. By the end of the century Bickerton House was almost without competition in Birkdale Park as a senior boys' school.

It is clear that many boys spent only their early years in Birkdale before moving on elsewhere. There was a local tradition of preparatory schools. In 1881, 62% per cent of 144 boys boarding within the Park were under the age of fourteen. This preparatory tradition was continued with the opening, in 1902, of Terra Nova, hard by the Birkdale Golf Club links. The name suggests the background of the promoter. Edwin Owen was born in Newfoundland, from where his father exported fish to Bristol. He did not follow in the family business, and after taking a mathematics degree at Cambridge he became a teacher. He was attracted to Birkdale by its reputation for health and built his school in the tall sand-dunes beyond the southern margin of the built-up area. The school was very expensive, and specialised in preparing boys for public schools and the navy. Unlike many private school promoters Owen apparently made no attempt to ingratiate himself with parents. He would not brook their interference, and visits were limited to official occasions. He did, however, virtually guarantee success in the Common Entrance Examination to Public Schools, and it was many years before a Terra Nova boy failed at this hurdle.

The original building was substantial, and success led to further additions.

Brighthelmston School.

Terra Nova School, c. 1908.

Set in five and a half acres of playing fields, which were enclosed by a five foot high perimeter wall, it became a large and lavishly equipped preparatory school. It had a workshop, an indoor heated swimming pool, gymnasium and shooting range. (The campus is now occupied by the Birkdale School for Children with Impaired Hearing.) A former pupil recalled that:

> Owen . . . was very health minded . . . the windows were always open. They were fitted with glass shields to direct the draughts upwards. The dormitories were spacious . . . one wash basin per boy.[29]

Some former pupils of Southport private schools have written of the physical privations of boarders and the wretched food they received. Old boys of Terra Nova recall that, although their food was anything but sumptious, Owen did eat with them and share it.

Terra Nova quickly established a reputation as a high-class preparatory school. The green and white caps conferred a social cachet on the wearer. Owen paid his pupils the princely sum of five shillings each time they could recover a Terra Nova cap from the unworthy head of an errand boy. A successful, if idiosyncratic schoolmaster, Owen must have been a forceful presence when he was elected to the Birkdale Council.

By 1911 there was a second much smaller "Preparatory School for Gentlemen's Sons" run by Miss Pacey at 22 Weld Road. One old boy of Terra Nova had no doubts about the social ranking of Birkdale Park's three boys' schools: "We considered ourselves vastly superior to Bickerton House or Miss Pacey's."

BIRKDALE PARK AT PRAYER

St. James' C.E. Church

Market forces ensured that Birkdale Park was extravagantly served with educational and medical facilities. It did not, however, enjoy similar riches in ecclesiastical provision. Swift's replacement as vicar, in 1874, was Robert Stephenson, a curate from Birmingham, who apparently owed his selection, from a long list of candidates, to a chance visit of one of the trustees when he was preaching.

Stephenson was an exceptional preacher, but he was an Evangelical who favoured the plain unadorned services of the Reformed Church of England. He preferred services to be said rather than sung in the "cathedral style", and he was strongly opposed to ritual and services constructed on Catholic principles. Indeed he objected to being called parish priest. Not surprisingly, he had close links with local Nonconformists. His distaste for Catholic influences extended to the appearance of the church. Not for him ornamentation and stained-glass windows. No such gifts were accepted during his incumbency. In fact, in 1889 a deputation of parishioners went over his head and unsuccessfully approached the Bishop, asking for approval for the installation of a carved reredos. Shortly after Stephenson had arrived in Birkdale, there had been a strong movement to demolish and replace the much criticised building. Thomas Docksey, the vicar's warden, offered to start a fund for a new church on a more central site, south of Weld Road, with a donation of £1,000. The offer was declined and Docksey, who favoured a sung service, resigned.

Stephenson opposed bazaars and what he described as Papal ways of raising money, believing that parishioners should donate freely to their church; and he frequently criticised the rich of Birkdale Park for not giving in proportion to their wealth. The evidence indicates that many Birkdale Park residents continued to attend churches in Southport, including a minority who went as far as St. Luke's for an Anglo-Catholic service.

Sticking to his principles, Stephenson was able to raise sufficient money to undertake some alterations to the church. It is interesting to note that St. James' did not have any parish rooms. In 1892, one parishioner pressed hard for some social functions. He believed that the congregation lacked "esprit de corps" from having no opportunity to draw together, or to raise funds. He went on to argue that every church in Southport had an annual reunion, and that if a "tea party" was not appropriate for aristocratic Birkdale Park they could have a dinner. Stephenson opposed this initiative but, interestingly, some ten years later the wardens did arrange a well-attended "Congregational Reunion" at the Palace Hotel. The promoters declared that its purpose was to enable the members of the congregation to become better acquainted, as there had been few opportunities over the years. There was no reference to Stephenson's presence in newspaper reports of this function. Stephenson appeared to be genuinely puzzled by the attitude of his parishioners. He said that he was unable to catch the warm sympathy which parishioners seemed to give to their clergy in Southport. He described the population of Birkdale as unsettled and fluctuating and difficult to unite. Nevertheless, his preaching was much admired, and he did build up the attendance at St. James', particularly for morning services.

There appears to have been a strong case for a second Anglican church at the south end of Birkdale Park, but there was not the financial support which would have enabled St. James' to sponsor such a development. Bishop Chavasse identified the symptoms of problems in the parish, in his address at the induction of the new vicar – Canon Hodgkin – in 1905, without attempting publicly to diagnose the causes. He declared that, for its size, the parish contained more men and women of culture, wealth and leisure than almost any other in the diocese. He went on to say that the size and nature of the church did not bear any proportion to the wealth of the people who worshipped in it.

He also noted that it might be necessary to build a second church in the sandhills to serve the new property.

Under Hodgkin, changes appear to have come quickly. A parish magazine was launched; parishioners started to donate memorial stained-glass windows and other ornamental items; and a fund for building improvements was well supported.

Trafalgar Road Congregational Church

The newer part of Birkdale Park, around Grosvenor Road, did not get a church, but oddly it did have a chapel. In 1878 the members of Southport's West End Congregational Church decided to support a chapel in this growing district. They paid £700 for a building at the corner of Trafalgar Road, opposite to the Smedley Hydro, and a further £500 to repair it. Thirteen members of West End transferred to the new chapel to give it an initial boost. At this time, the chapel was on the outer fringe of the built-up area, and it struggled to survive. Served by a succession of pastors, it owed its continuing existence to financial support from other Congregational chapels in Southport.

The chapel experienced a change in fortune towards the end of the century. A new Pastor, the Rev. H. Boyden, played a significant role. He spoke of his small but united congregation being sociable and energetic. Even more influential, however, was the Rev. Fred Smith, a retired minister resident in Westbourne Road, who was a leading member of the Birkdale Liberal party and a Chairman of the Local Council. One of the principal financial backers was the radical Ryley family who lived at the corner of Grosvenor Road, opposite the chapel. Perhaps the most significant factor in its improved fortune was the expansion of middle-class housing on the other side of the railway. The level-crossing on Grosvenor Road meant that the chapel was coveniently situated to serve this area. In addition to being the only Congregational chapel in Birkdale, it also carried the prestige and respectability of being within the 'Park'. In 1905 Smith laid the foundation stone for a new chapel costing £4,000. The chapel was in the late decorated style, built in patent brick with Bath stone dressing. The old chapel was used for a Sunday School.

St. Joseph's R.C. Church

Supported by the squire, the financially secure Roman Catholic church of St. Joseph's appeared to enjoy relatively serene progress. It presented a much lower profile than its Protestant neighbours, attracting little publicity beyond accounts of fashionable weddings and funerals – except for a court case in 1889, when a prayer book belonging to Miss Chamberlain (a 'Frontager') was stolen from the church. A local girl was charged with sacrilege and gaoled for two months.

Sport was a dominant feature of Victorian public school life, and cricket was a fashionable game. Birkdale Park followed the example of other socially superior residential Merseyside suburbs, such as Blundellsands and Sefton Park, in supporting a cricket club. Southport Cricket Club had played on a pitch off York Road in the late 1850s, but the rapid spread of housing had led to it moving to a ground in Southport. Although there are reports of a Birkdale Park Cricket Club playing as early as 1865, the foundation, in 1874, of the Birkdale Cricket Club coincided with the formation of the Birkdale Park Land Company, which gave the club a seven-year lease on a four and a half acre plot.[30] The ground was outside the prevailing margin of building, and the Company expected that the Club would later be re-housed in the park, for which Weld-Blundell had offered the Local Board 50 acres, thus releasing the Trafalgar Road site for more lucrative development. As the Board turned down the offer of a park, the Club had to negotiate for the purchase of the Trafalgar Road ground. The price – £550 – was very reasonable when compared with the Company's charges for building land, but it still yielded a handsome profit. To finance the deal the Birkdale Cricket Club Ground Company was formed, with a 1,000 £1 shares. Although less than half were taken, the Company took a mortgage and the ground was secured. One of the shareholders, George Chamberlain, a 'Frontager' whose five sons played for the team, was the Club's first President. Local schoolmasters, such as the Mathwins, figured prominently amongst the players.

The pavilion was built ". . . in Queen Anne style with quaint windows"; the *Southport Visiter* described it as ". . . one of the best buildings of its kind we have ever seen." In the early days there was a 3d admission charge for spectators ". . . ladies will, of course, be free." In 1902, the club combined with the Southport Cricket Club. The Birkdale Club's benefactors included James Mulgrew, who lived on the corner of Waterloo Road and Grosvenor Road, and George Kilvert who lived at 'Brecken-le-Dale', opposite the ground. Kilvert was also a member of the Birkdale Council and the Lancashire County Council, whilst Mulgrew was a councillor and the President of the Birkdale Liberal Association. Wealthy men, they were typical of the residents of the large mansions which were appearing to the south of Grosvenor Road. Not surprisingly both were also members of Birkdale Golf Club.

Like cricket, golf was a socially acceptable game. Blundellsands, Liverpool's northern suburb, had its West Lancashire Golf Club; whilst Southport Golf Club, serving the affluent Hesketh Park district of Southport, was formed in 1885. Golf was a fashionable sport, and a group of Birkdale Park residents got together to consider forming a club. Their first meeting, in 1889, was held in the Weld Road home of J.C. Barrett, J.P., a Chairman of the Birkdale Urban District Council. Charles Weld-Blundell offered them ground between Birkdale Common and the expanding working-class dormitory of New Birkdale, an area that now includes Bedford Park. This might seem to be an unusual choice, when the rash of golf courses being built on the Lancashire coast were being located adjacent to middle-class residential areas. In Birkdale, Thomas Weld-Blundell had previously sold much of his land west of the railway to the Birkdale Park Land Company, and Charles had ambitions for a substantial middle-class, residential estate inland of the railway, on land which he still owned. Perhaps he hoped that the presence of a golf course would stimulate this development.

The Birkdale Golf Club course was some way from the Birkdale Park homes of the members and, in the absence of a clubhouse, they used accommodation at the adjoining Portland Hotel.[31] Charles Weld-Blundell accepted the presidency of the Club. The first Honorary Secretary was a Westbourne Road resident and former 'Frontager', William Shatwell, a solicitor and member of the Birkdale Local Board. Contemporaries judged him to be the founder of the Club. Other early members included T.O. Clinning, the leader of Birkdale's Conservatives, and fellow councillor Thomas Docksey of Lulworth Road, who was a major shareholder of the Birkdale Park Land Company. W.H. Hayes, Honorary Secretary from 1896, was also a councillor, and all three were at one time chairman of the authority.

The approach to the course was via Bedford Road, which at this time had not been sewered and was frequently flooded. Even worse was the overflow from the nearby laundry, which was not efficiently drained. The nine-hole course had to be reorganised several times owing to the formation of new roads in the district. Not surprisingly, members believed that the insalubrious setting of the course was inhibiting the club's development. At the annual dinner in April 1894, they were told that the: ". . . grounds were unequal to requirements" and that the Club was actively seeking an alternative in the most beautiful spot in Birkdale, in the area between the two railways.[32] The considerable expense of fashioning a course among the tall dunes did not daunt these pioneers.

Despite delays in negotiations with Weld-Blundell, work started on preparing the new course in 1896, a year before agreement was finally reached. The Club was allowed the 190-acre site on a peppercorn rent during the first two years, and thereafter was charged an annual sum of £100. Although this return was derisory from the landowner's point of view, experience elsewhere had shown that the presence of a golf course had a very beneficial effect on the surrounding property. It acted as a great fertilizer for villa development. Nevertheless, Weld-Blundell restricted the Club's lease to 21 years, thus retaining flexibility in relation to future development of the land.

In order to develop the club the Birkdale Golf Links and Building Company was formed. By 1898 just over a third of the 190 members were shareholders, and £950 had been spent on the links and almost £600 on the clubhouse, which was reached from Lancaster Road.

Prior to the building of the golf course the nearest houses to the margin of the links were still several hundred yards away in Grosvenor Road, on Birkdale Park Land Company plots. The golf correspondent of the *Southport Visiter* claimed that it was the presence of the golf club that had enabled ". . . the Birkdale Park Land Company to declare a dividend unequalled in its annals."[33] On another occasion he reported that there was scarcely a home in a large district around the links where at least one member did not reside.

It transpired that, in error, the Club had built its pavilion outside the limits of the land which it had leased. There was no generosity of spirit and accommodation forthcoming from the Land Company, which now wanted the land for the development of its prospering estate. In 1904, having been given only very brief notice, the Club was required to demolish its clubhouse. The Club demonstrated its financial strength by immediately building a replacement, at a cost of £1,670.

Maps from the Weld-Blundell Estate Office show the area, which included the course, to be latticed by projected roads, and the club's short lease would have allowed an early reversion to the Estate. Fortunately for the Club these ambitious building plans were not realised, and the links survived to become "Royal" in 1951 and Birkdale's major claim to fame.

Birkdale Golf Club, c. 1908.

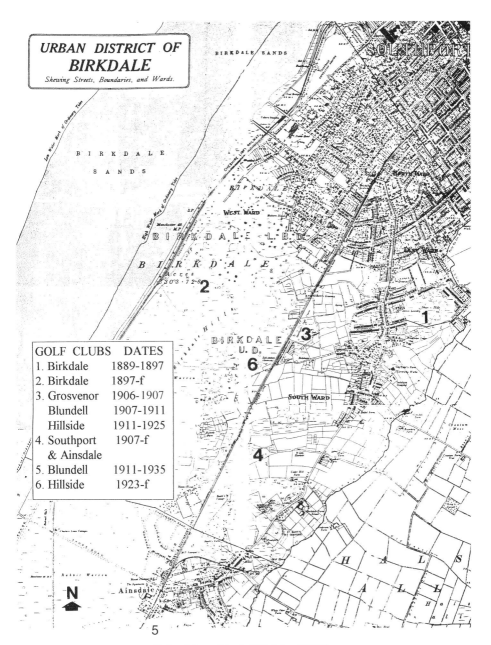

GOLF CLUBS   DATES
1. Birkdale   1889-1897
2. Birkdale   1897-f
3. Grosvenor   1906-1907
   Blundell   1907-1911
   Hillside   1911-1925
4. Southport   1907-f
   & Ainsdale
5. Blundell   1911-1935
6. Hillside   1923-f

Extract from 6 inch O.S. Map (1893).

The residents of Birkdale Park also enjoyed a fashionable tennis club. Records show that the Birkdale Lawn Tennis Club hired three courts in the grounds of the Palace Hotel in 1878. Their agreement also provided them with the use of two changing rooms and two toilets in the hotel. There were 43 members, with the men paying an annual subscription of 7s 6d and the ladies 5 shillings. Many of the members also belonged to the cricket and golf clubs. Notable personalities included J.C. Barrett, W.W.P. Shatwell, and George Chamberlain. Concerned about tenure at the Palace Hotel, the committee considered moving to the new Recreation Ground. Not surprisingly this socially elite club did not find it suitable.

The Club had originally been called the Birkdale Archery and Tennis Club. Facilities for archery had been available at the Palace from its inception. Archery within the Birkdale Club did not flourish to the extent of the tennis, which became an independent club. Although there is little evidence of a thriving local archery club, the hotel grounds became a regional centre for archery, and were the venue for the annual Grand Northern Archery Meeting.

Bowling was popular with all sections of Victorian society. Birkdale Park residents used the greens in the refined setting of the grounds of the Palace and Smedley Hotels. Additionally, Birkdale Bowling Club, the gentlemen's subscription club founded by Walter Smith, provided greens in Aughton Road. This club enjoyed luxurious premises and the membership, which was limited to 60, included many of Birkdale's leading personalities.

The Palace and Smedley Hotels also provided lawns for croquet. The Birkdale and Southport Croquet Club, founded in 1900, decided to play on Victoria Park. The Club applied to the Council for permission to erect a pavilion, but the Law Clerk advised the Council that it did not have the power to allow this. A way was found round this regulation and the pavilion, still a feature of the park, was opened in July 1904. It was described as a picturesque thatch-covered cottage with a capacious shaded verandah, directly overlooking the large lawn. The Club was paying the Council £40 a year for the hire of the facilities.

CHAPTER FIVE

NEW BIRKDALE: THE OTHER SIDE OF THE TRACK

It is true that the east, or business side, of the line has grown out of proportion to the west since 1871, but it is the wealth of the western which is responsible for the growth of the eastern.

J. Carr, Registrar of Birkdale, 1901

THE BEGINNINGS: A WORKING-CLASS DORMITORY

The Ecclesfield District

New Birkdale was not confined to the villas of affluent Birkdale Park: a very different community developed on the other side of the barrier provided by the railway line. It started as an overspill from the socially depressed Ecclesfield district of Southport. Ecclesfield was the Boundary Street area between Shakespeare Street and Sefton Street. Weld-Blundell allowed it to spread into Birkdale where a terrace of small cheap houses was built in Grove Street, an unmade road just inside the boundary. As in Birkdale Park, the blocking of the Boundary Brook by the Scarisbrick Estate had removed the traditional drainage channel for this area and led to flooding. The flooding of the cess pits on the small cramped plots threatened the purity of drinking water from the shallow wells, and led to a fear of cholera. In 1869, the average annual rental of the 28 houses in Grove Street was under £9, as was that in adjoining Fisher (now Fernley) Road. There were 54 small houses in Upper Aughton Road, but the rentals of from £10 to £16, with an average of £14, suggest that there were subtle variations in value and status within this area of low-value property.

As in Birkdale Park, houses in this part of New Birkdale were being built on what had been agricultural land. Initially the existing scattered cottages and farmhouses survived, although Birkdale's old wooden windmill, which was situated at the corner of Grove Street and Snuttering Lane (now Mosley Street), was pulled down in the 1860s. The erection of cheap houses did not continue deeper into Birkdale. Beyond Upper Aughton Road, in Alma Road and then Kent and Clarence Roads, more expensive superior dwellings were built for skilled tradesmen and lower middle-class families. These roads shared the early drainage problems. Indeed the pools in the pot-holes in Alma Road were so deep in winter, that pedestrians had to use planks to cross them. One builder claimed that unless the drainage was improved, he would only be able to let his houses in Kent Road ". . . to very humble people at low rents."[1] The average rentals in Kent and Clarence Roads, of between £16 and £17, maintained the social gradient away from the Southport boundary. The Birkdale Local Board was slow to adopt and to make roads in New Birkdale, and when it did it experienced difficulty in recovering payments from the house owners.

New Birkdale East of the Line: Estimated Annual Rental 1869

	No. of Houses	Ave. Rental	No. Over £25
Grove Street	28	£9	–
Fisher Road	6	£9	–
Upper Aughton Road	54	£14	–
Kent Road	16	£16	–
Clarence Road	6	£17	–
Railway Walk	23	£17	1
Alma Road	36	£21	7
Bolton Road	2	£30	2
Liverpool Road	42	£30	33

source: B.L.B. *General Rate Book 1869*

The Ecclesfield area was soon served by a public house – The Blundell Arms – built on the corner of Upper Aughton Road and Clarence Road. Billiard and bowls competitions were regularly held, with stakes and prizes being as high as £100. Archie Coke was the publican for 25 years, and frequently figured as the winner in bowling competitions. A greyhound trainer with a national reputation, Coke successfully prepared dogs for the Waterloo Cup. Behind the pub, he housed up to 60 dogs in well-designed kennels.

Inland Expansion: The Chatham Road District
A Birkdale resident recalled that in 1872: "From the Blundell Arms Hotel the open country stretched right away to the horizon, broken only by the villages of Halsall and Aughton."[2] In neighbouring Southport, the growth in population had led to the demolition of older cheap properties in the outskirts, in order to make way for better quality semi-detached dwellings. As a result,

those on the lower rungs of the working-class hierarchy – mainly labourers – had to move to cheaper property, which was being built even further out from the town centre. In Birkdale, the building of such dwellings occurred inland from Ecclesfield, along the boundary with Southport. By the early 1870s building reached what was to become the inland margin of Birkdale, where town met country in Chatham (later Compton) Road. Here some speculators indulged in "jerry" building: one Chatham Road house quickly collapsed as the foundations, such as they were, had been placed directly on undisturbed turf. A more responsible attitude to building was evident in the work of the Artizan Dwelling Company, which was formed as a benevolent local initiative to provide cheap sound houses for working-men. Walter Smith, who figured so prominently in the Birkdale Park Land Company and the Southport and Cheshire Lines Extension Railway Company, was this Company's chairman. The Artizan Dwelling Company complained bitterly to the Local Board about the state of the houses opposite its properties at the bottom end of Upper Aughton Road. The police had likened them to "Little Ireland", the infamous social blackspot to the north of Southport and, in 1877, the Company claimed that the overcrowding and social conditions were having a depressing effect on its properties – nine of its thirteen houses being empty. It was unfortunate that its initiative coincided with a severe recession in trade, which was accompanied by a glut of houses on the market. Eventually the Company did manage to let all its 32 houses, but at much reduced rentals, and subsequent financial problems led to its liquidation. Not surprisingly, the non-interventionist Birkdale Local Board, and its successor the Urban District Council, did not choose to build municipal houses and the provision of low-cost accommodation was left to the market.

By 1881 54 houses had been built in Chatham Road, of which only two were empty, and 31 plots were yet to be built on. Chatham Road was typical of the working-class districts of New Birkdale, in that the majority of workers were supplying services, many of them for the wealthy residents of Birkdale Park. The census shows five working-women as heads of households: four were entered as "laundress", and one as a "charwoman". Of the male heads of household, there were twelve tradesmen, mostly in the building industry, five building labourers, two gardeners and a cab driver. There were also two farm labourers, a cow-keeper and a dairyman. Providing services for the residents of the immediate area were a beerseller/grocer and a beerhouse-keeper.

Only two heads of household had been born in Birkdale – John Formby, a labourer, and Mary Rimmer, a widowed laundress. In addition there were seven others who were born in Southport. Although the remainder were born in many parts of the United Kingdom, the place of birth of their children shows that the majority had migrated from Southport to New Birkdale. Such local movement was very different to the pattern in Birkdale Park.

Householders in working-class dormitories such as this were not normally servant-keepers. An exception in Chatham Road was William Johnson, a cow-keeper, who lived with his wife and two young children, and the household included a fifteen-year-old local girl as a general servant.

Reporting to the Board in 1888, the Medical Officer was selective in his use of evidence and contrived to put a favourable gloss on the conditions obtaining in this part of New Birkdale. He stated that:

> . . . the smaller cottage property is either detached or semi-detached and situated in open healthy spaces looking over agricultural land.[3]

It was true that, unlike their terraced counterparts in many northern towns, all the houses in Birkdale had at least some garden, and true also that Chatham Road and Stamford Road were situated on the margin of the agricultural hinterland; nevertheless, the Officer's bland statement hardly conveyed the squalor of their urban reality. Early failure to link these dwellings to Birkdale's developing sewerage system, and the close proximity of the settling tanks and filter beds for this system, which were situated alongside Chatham Road, meant that the area was frequently subjected to foul stenches. Doctors regularly treated members of local families for what was described as "sewer throat". Memorials of complaint to the Birkdale Local Board which were signed by up to 140 householders did not, however, carry the weight of those emanating from Birkdale Park's 'Frontagers'.

The widespread Birkdale custom of keeping pigs added to the area's environmental problems. In the absence of piped drainage, slimy pits became a feature of the neighbourhood. It was estimated that there were over 600 pigs being kept in back gardens in and around Chatham Road, with as many as 50 at one house. The Medical Officer frequently complained about this practice, but local politicians were reluctant to alienate Birkdale's many pig-keepers. Conditions in this area were further exacerbated by the presence of slaughter houses. In 1878, the Medical Officer complained of one belonging to Mr. Hulme being ". . . a most foul and abominable nuisance, and very dangerous to public health."[4] It seems that all the waste was thrown to decay in a cess pit, which drained into a ditch.

Outbreaks of diphtheria and typhoid fever led to the Medical Officer progressively closing drinking wells. Even after the area was supplied with town water in the kitchens, some householders had it cut off at the main because of the expense, and persisted in using water from polluted wells.

As late as 1884, the roadway of Chatham Road consisted of just a narrow paved cart track set in the centre of a sea of sand. There were no pavements or curbs, and pedestrians were thus obliged to walk in the middle of the road. These conditions were severely criticised by the coroner when a young child was killed by a cart.

Overcrowding was certainly prevalent. In 1889, William Warburton, agitating for a bigger Board School, claimed:

> In six small houses in Chatham Road – with three small rooms each downstairs, one about eleven feet square, a kitchen about the same size, and a scullery about seven or eight feet square, with three corresponding rooms upstairs – I have been told that in these six little houses, which are tenanted at six shillings a week each, including rates, which the owners pay, one hundred to one hundred and twenty men, women and children dwell.[5]

Warburton, a Liberal firebrand, who was one of the principal supporters of Board School education in Birkdale, was prone to exaggerate his case; the Medical Officer visited the six houses and found only 47 people. It was later discovered that in one house there was a total of eighteen residents from three families. The Census Enumerator had no axe to grind in such political/statistical battles and his returns, taken eight years earlier, show that the six most crowded houses in Chatham Road contained 60 residents, with eleven being the maximum in one of these tiny cottages. Overcrowding continued to be an issue, and in extreme cases the Council wrote to the householder.

It was also in 1889 that a "Baby Farming Scandal" surfaced in Chatham Road. A stone mason's labourer and his wife had been taking in ("farming") illegitimate children, at a charge of 6s a week. They were prosecuted after three of the babies had died. It seems that the youngsters had been incarcerated in a bedroom, and were caked with layer upon layer of excrement, whilst the bedding was alive with maggots. The babies had been given wine and laudanum in attempts to pacify them. The couple were found guilty of manslaughter and sentenced to penal servitude. A direct outcome of the case was the establishment of a local office of the N.S.P.C.C.[6] Further prosecutions against local parents, both for neglect and for abandoning children, were brought by the Society.

Although there was no infirmary in Birkdale, the Local Board did have a statutory obligation to provide a hospital for infectious cases. In 1877 it bought two small houses for this purpose – numbers 37 and 39 Swire (now Matlock) Road, close to Chatham Road. At this time they stood alone in what was a thinly populated area, but rapid urban growth transformed it into the most densely populated district of Birkdale. In an attempt to meet the health needs of this crowded neighbourhood the Birkdale Provident Dispensary was set up at 33 Swire Road in 1879. Several members of the Local Board were supporters of this philanthropic venture and the Board's Medical Officer was amongst the doctors who gave their services. Later the Provident Society provided two almshouses – 29 and 37 Eastbourne Road – where eight elderly ladies, between the ages of 70 and 80, were able to look after themselves in their own rooms. The Society also maintained a further two houses – 49 and 53 Eastbourne Road

– ". . . for the reception of those who have seen better times, but have just sufficient for their maintenance."[7] Birkdale residents unable to support themselves would come under the aegis of the Poor Law Guardians and could well end up in the work-house, at Ormskirk – the ultimate social humiliation which was greatly feared by many old and poor people living in this part of New Birkdale.

The Chatham Road neighbourhood was undoubtedly an area of social deprivation. It provided the cheapest housing to be had in the area. Conditions were not as bad, however, as those to be found in the most depressed areas of other northern towns and cities. Also, the majority of the inhabitants were in work, although the dominance of the building trade, with its vulnerability to the vagaries of both the market and weather, meant that periods of widespread unemployment were common. The normal rate for a joiner was about 4d an hour, giving a wage of £2 for a 50-hour week. Both tradesmen and labourers were laid off when there was no work, and the problems were exacerbated by the fact that employers paid lower wages during the winter months, when labour was in plentiful supply. Harsh winters invariably led to the setting up of soup kitchens in the district by churches, individuals and the local police. In 1879, the Medical Officer reported that the distress had not had an adverse effect upon health ". . . owing mainly to the admirable manner in which the urgent wants of the poor have been supplied by the rich."[8]

Providing services continued to be the principal occupation for householders in this part of New Birkdale. The 1891 census returns show twelve tradesmen living in Chatham Road, of whom five were painters. The proportion of labourers was falling as the growth of the conurbation was forcing members of this group to move further out to even cheaper housing on Birkdale Common. The labourers still living in Chatham Road included five working in building trades, seven gardeners and seven involved in transporting goods and passengers. There were also three blacksmiths and a "practical engineer". There is evidence to show that, by the turn of the century, there was some easement in the social deprivation that characterised the early years in Chatham Road. By 1910, labourers constituted less than a third of the heads of household, whilst the proportion of tradesmen had increased. Also, there were a number of businesses being conducted in the yards behind the road. Thomas Ormesher ran his builder's business from number 2, and also owned four other cottages in the neighbourhood. Walter Manning, of Kew Road, built Birkdale's first ambulance at his Chatham Road carriage works. His son Percy distinguished himself at the Board School, being awarded one of the first local authority scholarships to attend Bootle Grammar School. Down another entry Messrs Mook and Co. manufactured mineral waters.

Upper Aughton Road was an important link road for New Birkdale. For residents of the Chatham Road district it provided a route to work, giving access to Birkdale Park and Southport. Initially this route was only available during the week, as the gates at the railway crossing were kept locked on Sundays. Upper Aughton Road became the spine of the early New Birkdale community east of the railway line. It contained the area's only fully licensed public house – the Blundell Arms. After the death of Archie Coke, in 1890, he was succeeded as licensee by his son John, who also carried on his sporting interests and trained a winner of the Waterloo Cup. By this time Upper Aughton Road contained nine other licensed premises, mostly off-licences. It also housed two breweries – Crown Brewery, which produced "Birkdale Bitter", and Victoria Brewery.

The west end of Upper Aughton Road developed as a neighbourhood shopping centre. As early as 1868, the *Johnson and Green Guide* showed a handful of shops around the Alma Road corner. On the opposite side, terraces of small cottages were built behind those fronting onto the road. As the population increased, many of the front cottages were replaced by shops. By 1881 there were three grocers, a butcher, a greengrocer, a beerseller, a wine and spirit merchant, and a newsagent. In 1898, the houses in Athol Terrace were converted into five shops. After having had his Chinese laundry in Everton Road closed by the Council, Mr. Sing's removal to Upper Aughton Road was greeted by a petition of protest signed by 87 residents. Despite this initial opposition the laundry remained, and survived until modern times.

The roads leading south from Upper Aughton Road – Everton Road, Kent Road and Alma Road – were socially superior to the roads in the Chatham Road neighbourhood. In 1869, the average rental in Alma Road was as high as £21, with seven houses rated at over £25. In 1871 over a third of the 37 householders in Alma Road were women living on an unearned income; ten years later this group constituted just under a quarter of the 42 residents; whilst in 1891 it numbered 21 out of 49. There were also nine retired men in 1871, fifteen in 1881, and thirteen in 1891. Several of Birkdale's small business-men chose to live in Alma Road. These included: John Goulder, the coach proprietor who had previously lived alongside his stables in Weld Road; James Shepherd, a coal merchant and Registrar of Births, Marriages and Deaths, who was also a long-serving member of the Birkdale Local Board; and Anne Parr, who was a butcher. It was ". . . on the shavings in a joiner's shop in Alma Road" that the Birkdale Liberal Club was founded in 1883, an indication of the appeal of Liberalism inland of the railway. Donations from Liberals living in Birkdale Park enabled the Club to move into rooms in Eastbourne Road.[9]

Under a half of the householders in Alma Road kept resident servants. In 1871 there was no household with more than one servant, and two of these servants were young girls of only twelve and thirteen. By 1881, two households included two servants, and ten years later only thirteen of the 49 households included a servant. The evidence suggests that Alma Road was an area of respectability and gentility without affluence. Unlike Chatham Road, the residents were not born locally, neither did they appear to have moved in from Southport. John Pye, a book-keeper, was the only householder born in Birkdale.

Social hierarchies were much more than statistical abstractions, later produced by historians. The residents had a deeply ingrained sense of class and knew their "station". Where a person lived was a very important element in a complex social pattern. There were variations in social status within as well as between roads. Residents had clear perceptions of the social superiority of one end or side of a road over the other. Even within terraces there were variations between end and centre houses.

Although there were no large manufacturers in Birkdale a few small enterprises flourished. William Lea of 55 Everton Road, a former editor of *Feathered World*, made bantam houses and runs. He received royal patronage when one of his houses was purchased for the estate at Sandringham. As a result his premises became "The Royal Appliance Works". He extended his range to include incubators. Bicycles were made by the Ribble Cycle Works in Liverpool Road. Number 46 Alma Road became the manual exchange for the Birkdale telephone system, provided by the National Telephone Company.

CHURCHES, CHAPELS AND SCHOOLS

The rapid development of New Birkdale, east of the railway, meant the presence of a growing number of working-class children, who would require elementary school places. The children of parents whose houses had an annual rental of more than £25 were not considered to be potential elementary school pupils. The middle classes were expected to fund and be responsible for the schooling of their own children. The Education Act of 1870 required that in each School District, of which Birkdale became one, there was an adequate provision of elementary school places.

Initially Birkdale children had crossed the boundary to attend one of Southport's many church schools. The nearest schools for east Birkdale's Catholic children were distant St. Marie's on the Sands, at the north end of Southport, and Sacred Heart in Ainsdale. A clause in the deeds of St. Joseph's Roman Catholic Church, in Birkdale Park, prevented the building of a school on this site. The peace of a high-class residential area, such as Birkdale Park was not to be disturbed by the presence of noisy and dirty elementary school scholars. As an alternative Thomas Weld-Blundell, the Roman Catholic landowner, granted a rent-free site for a school-chapel, which was built at the

Vaughan Road.

St. Joseph's/St. Teresa's R.C. School.

corner of Everton Road and Vaughan Road in 1869. This was conveniently located for the families who would use it. The school was closely linked to the Weld Road house of the Sisters of Notre Dame, and over the years many of the teachers were resident sisters.[10]

Protestant children had either to make the long walk over the Common to the village school, or cross the boundary with Southport to attend schools run by St. Paul's or the Trinity Wesleyan church. From 1864 Francis Cooper, a young curate in the parish of St. Paul's, had been working in its Ecclesfield district and had built a small mission church on the Southport side of the boundary. Backed by Charles Hesketh, the Rector of North Meols, Cooper became a curate of St. James' and vicar-designate for a new parish to serve east Birkdale. This was brought into being with the blessing of Swift, the vicar of St. James'. The new parish – St. Peter's – consisted of a half mile deep strip inland of the railway, extending from the original Birkdale railway station at Barlow's Crossing to Duke Street, just within Southport. An unsuccessful approach was made to Weld-Blundell for the donation of a building site, and it was the energy and drive of Cooper that led to the opening of a school-church on the corner opposite the Blundell Arms. This building is now the headquarters of the local A.T.C. unit.

Having built the school-church in Upper Aughton Road the Rev. Cooper set about collecting funds for a parish church. The first donation to his appeal was a contribution of half-a-crown from a local charwoman, whilst the most substantial – £1,000 – was made by William Atkinson, the Southport philanthropist who is principally remembered for his gift of the library and art gallery. The church was opened in 1872 on a site at the centre of the parish, on the corner of Claremont Road. Costing about £2,400, it was faced with stone from Appley Bridge and a contemporary described it as a ". . . pretty little Gothic building."[11]

Cooper was not prepared to live in the shadow of St. James' in Birkdale Park, and he objected to Swift's successor, Stephenson, continuing to use what he believed was the now redundant title of Vicar of Birkdale. After the two vicars exchanged sharp letters in the local press, the matter was referred to the Diocese. The outcome was that they agreed to adopt the titles of Vicar of St. James' Birkdale, and Vicar of St. Peter's Birkdale respectively.

Under the influence of Cooper, an energetic and campaigning vicar, St. Peter's Vestry Meetings became a lively forum for social protest. Cooper complained bitterly about the condition of the roads around the new church. The members of the Vestry embarrassed the Local Board with their vehement declarations that their side of the railway line was losing out in public spending.

When St. Peter's parish was brought into being it contained only 137 inhabited houses; ten years later this number had risen to 1161. Although the parish included a large proportion of the artizan classes, there was an

St. Peter's C.E. Church.

increasing number of middle-class residents, living mainly to the south of the church. In 1869 there were 42 houses in Liverpool Road, with estimated annual rents averaging about £30. More than three-quarters of them were rated at over £25. Although not of the size and grandeur of the villas in Birkdale Park, the building of superior middle-class dwellings continued inland in an arc away from the railway station, Bolton Road and Crosby Road providing examples.

Wesleyan Methodists had been holding cottage services in the district since 1858. The accommodation soon proved to be inadequate for the growing congregation and Ecclesfield Chapel was built. This building, which still serves as a chapel, was just across the boundary in Southport, on the corner of what is now Fernley Road. Very plain in character, the entire cost of the building was less than £150. There was no heating, and music was provided by a double bass and a cello. The Birkdale Wesleyan congregation soon outgrew Ecclesfield Chapel and, following the demolition of four cottages, Wesley Church was opened in 1872 on the corner of Upper Aughton Road and Kent Road. This fine new church had accommodation for 600 people and the entire cost – £4,000 for the building plus £700 for the site – was borne by John Fernley of 'Clairville'. This was the most substantial philanthropic gesture from a Birkdale Park resident for a Birkdale cause. The cost was more than double that of St. James'.

97

Wesley Kent Road Methodist Church.

The church's style was Early English and its grey stone provided a contrast to the surrounding brick-built dwellings. Although he personally supervised the building, Fernley did not cross the railway line to attend this east Birkdale church. He was a member of the fashionable Trinity Wesleyan church in Southport's Duke Street, which he had built earlier. The new Wesley Church drew much of its support from its immediate surrounds and from the superior property to its south.

Not surprisingly, the social problems of the Chatham Road neighbourhood attracted missionary support. In 1879 a United Methodist Free Chapel was built in Chatham Road. The site, opposite to Bury Road, is now used for commercial purposes. The chapel was built at a cost of about £900 as a Home Mission Station by the prosperous United Methodist Church in Southport's Duke Street (now the Masonic Hall). There were frequent changes of pastor, and on several occasions the Mission was threatened by closure. Its survival owed much to the financial support and leadership of T. Rushworth, a Liberal Councillor. Perhaps the Chapel's greatest success was its very large Sunday School.

There was a second mission room in the neighbourhood in premises in Broome Road (off Chatham Road) which were owned by the redoubtable Kate Ryley. It was used principally for the Broome Road P.S.A. (Pleasant Sunday

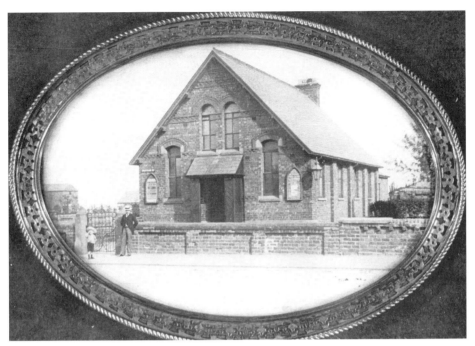

Chatham Road United Methodist Free Chapel.

Afternoon) group, a weekly religious meeting for women, which featured a speaker and a singer. Miss Ryley, the president, was the driving force behind this group. Kate Ryley was an ardent advocate of the cause of women's emancipation, and although she was not a suffragette she supported them. Her interests were wide: she urged women to join the anti-war movement, highlighting the excessive number of deaths of Boer women and children in concentration camps; she deplored the exploitation of Chinese labourers, and the plurality of wives in Africa; she also actively campaigned against bull-fighting in Spain.

In St. Peter's parish there was a dramatic increase in the amount of low-cost housing being built at the inland margin of the township during the early 1880s. Development continued along Stamford Road and Kew Road. Much of the land was far from suitable for building. Several houses were erected on peat, which provided poor foundations. Houses were built without drainage or piped water. For some, there were not even wells available and the residents used water from the ditches in the adjoining fields. Much of the property in Stamford Road was built by Mr. E. Herbert, who had come to live in the road and decided to invest some £3000 in the neighbourhood.[12] In 1883 the vicar of

St. Peter's, the Rev. F. Cooper, wrote:

> The inhabitants are mostly cottagers, who have been compelled to migrate there in consequence of the destruction in Southport of the small dwelling houses in which they formerly resided. Their houses have been pulled down in order to make room for the erection of better classes of houses, and they have found Birkdale habitations suited to their needs.[13]

Cooper's response was to create a mission church. He recruited Edwin Collier, a 17-year-old from Wigan waiting to go to Cambridge, to undertake this work and the mission opened in temporary accommodation at the corner of Bedford Road and Kew Road. Later, in 1883 a new Mission (St. Aidan's) was opened in Kew Road.

The Birkdale Methodists adopted a similar strategy. As early as 1876 members of Wesley Church had held cottage meetings in Stamford Road. This was largely the initiative of Mrs. Fynney, an elderly lady who had lived in South Africa. Two cottages were combined to form a small mission church. In 1884, Dr. James Wood, a mayor of Southport and a prominent Methodist, laid the foundation stone for a new mission church on Brighton Road, at the corner with Kew Road. The 500-seat chapel cost some £1500 to build. The church was adjoined by well-used schoolrooms catering for a range of activities. These included a small library, which Kate Ryley optimistically described as ". . . a stepping stone to a Birkdale Library", a cause for which she enthusiastically campaigned and to which she generously subscribed.[14]

The rapid increase in the population in the Chatham Road neighbourhood meant that there were many more children requiring elementary school places. When, in 1883, the Government's Education Department warned about a shortage of accommodation, the Birkdale Park parishioners of St. Joseph's immediately built a new schoolroom, providing more than sufficient places for local Catholic children.[15] The school also served as a chapel-of-ease and was consecrated as St. Teresa's, the saint whose name was borne by Thomas Weld-Blundell's wife. A handsome new church was given by his son Charles Weld-Blundell in 1898. The largely working-class Anglican Parish of St. Peter's was not so favourably placed to respond. It had taken three years to pay off the initial cost of building the school, and in response to increased pressure a new classroom, providing a further 90 places, had been built in 1881. The relatively poor parish had also faced the expense of setting up its mission church in Kew Road.

If the churches could not supply sufficient school places the 1870 Education Act required that a locally elected school board should be set up. In 1883 the Inspector declared that this part of Birkdale had a massive deficiency of 453 places. How could this be? The fact was that many children from east Birkdale attended schools in adjoining Southport, where there was an abundance of school places. These schools were convenient for Birkdale children, but

Southport was a separate School District. In addition, regular school attendance was still avoided by many Birkdale children.

It was only at this late hour that the complacent Birkdale Local Board began to treat the threat of the imposition of a school board, with its consequent charge on the rates, as important. Deputations were sent to the Education Department in London, but to no avail. An ad-hoc committee of ratepayers was set up to try to find additional school places within the Birkdale School District. St. Peter's decided that they could do no more and the hopes of the committee rested on the Wesleyans. Wesley Church, in Upper Aughton Road, had magnificent new schoolrooms for its Sunday School. The committee sought to influence the trustees to open these premises as a day school. The facilities would have provided accommodation in excess of the deficiency, and of a quality unequalled by any of the Birkdale elementary schools. Unfortunately for the Board, the Wesleyans showed no inclination to allow their schoolrooms to be used. A supporter argued that:

> All the children of the respectable poor are now being educated; but there are many uncared for wastrels who must also go to school . . . the daily invasion of the rougher elements of Birkdale would make the rooms uninhabitable.[16]

In fact the Wesleyans had a large half-empty day school at Talbot Street, in Southport. Birkdale children provided a substantial proportion of the children attending this school and the Birkdale Wesleyans did not wish ". . . to compete or incur the expense of an extra school."

Time ran out and the Order for a School Board was issued. Unlike some large urban authorities which had welcomed the arrival of a School Board, a reluctant Birkdale was dragged kicking and screaming into this position. The composition of the first School Board was agreed without an election. The Birkdale establishment took it over. At a later election, a Birkdale working man offered himself as a candidate. He was a joiner living in Vaughan Road, and the father of a child attending the Board School. He failed to secure election, coming bottom of the poll. Religious allegiance proved to be the critical variable in determining the composition of the School Board. There was a compact of Anglican and Roman Catholic members which dominated the first and subsequent Boards. Not surprisingly, they supported their own church schools rather than that of the Board, of which they were members. This majority was savagely attacked by a progressive minority on the Board. They accused them of ". . . starving Board School education and providing a feeding bottle for denominationalism in Birkdale." It was argued that:

> Their interests do not lie with the School Board but with the propping up of denominational schools at the expense of the ratepayers.[17]

Conflict was present from the Board's inception. The progressives campaigned for a Board School with accommodation for 600, whilst the majority talked in terms of a school for 450. Each side produced contradictory statistical evidence to support its case. In the end the government Education Department approved the erection of a school to accommodate 490 children. The school (now Birkdale County Primary) was built on a site at the corner of Bury and Matlock Roads. Members of the progressive minority, who were enthusiastic supporters of non-denominational board schools, wanted the pomp and ceremony of an official public opening. The prevailing view of the voluntaryist majority was that the quieter they could make the opening the better.

The new school rapidly filled, and bitter controversy over its size continued to dominate the Board. William Warburton, of Regent Road, was the scourge of the complacent majority. He fanned the flames of controversy and frequently used the correspondence columns of the local newspapers to press his case. The accommodation issue came to a head when, the Board having ignored a warning from the Inspector to provide more accommodation, the Education Department withheld payment of the annual grant which constituted a considerable proportion of the school's income. The majority on the Board were not immediately cowed by this drastic act, but the threat of having to increase local rates in order to make up for lost government grant compelled them, albeit reluctantly, to take action. Extensions, adding a further 421 places, were opened in 1892.

The task of enforcing attendance proved to be a problem and the School Board, with its Attendance Officer, was responsible for this aspect in all Birkdale's elementary schools. Initially, Birkdale parents treated this issue in a rather cavalier fashion. The Attendance Committee reported that only five out of seventeen parents summoned to attend one of their meetings put in an appearance: "The parents seemed to pay no heed to warning notices and of the five who did appear two had had more to drink than was good for them."[18] The Board started to prosecute parents in the magistrate's court and to have persistently bad attenders placed in the Hightown Truant School. In an attempt to reinforce the authority of the Attendance Officers, they were issued with tall military-style hats. Many pupils of the new Board School had only recently been forced into attending school at all, and had not formed habits of regular attendance. The Attendance Officer reported that: ". . . the worst attenders lived in Chatham Road and the furthest end of Upper Aughton Road."

Arthur Mortimer, the headmaster of Birkdale Board School, frequently identified the impoverished social background of the children as an explanation for poor attendance and the modest educational achievements of the children:

> Another cause of difficulty is the extreme poverty of a great many of the people living in the district. Chatham Road, Stamford Road, Kew Road, Broome Road, etc. – whence most of our children come – are inhabited by people in the poorest of circumstances. Many of the people residing in the district . . . are in a great measure migratory – the poor moving in search of work.[19]

Although there is some truth in such statements, the headmaster would be tempted to exaggerate in order to influence the Board.

From the school's first year, Mortimer had faced problems relating to corporal punishment. There were many complaints from parents concerning a lady teacher who persistently boxed children's ears. One parent complained that she had ". . . boxed her daughter's ears until they bled."[20] The head reported that the teacher was ". . . in the habit of daily and repeatedly during the day boxing children's ears," and that ". . . many of the children suffer earache and headache owing to this treatment." The Board passed a rule limiting the use of corporal punishment to the headteacher. In the late 1890s this rule featured in a bitter controversy involving Kate Ryley, who had inherited Warburton's radical mantle as a fiery opponent of the majority on the Board. Ryley's attacks were focussed on Mortimer. In a long-running feud the pair indulged in the most vicious personal recriminations through the correspondence columns of the local papers. Kate Ryley frequently visited the school and attempted to interfere in its day-to-day running.

She and other members of the minority had long resented what they considered to be Mortimer's cavalier attitude towards them. Thus, when an unfavourable inspector's report presented an opportunity, they went for the jugular. The next election was fought on the headmastership issue, and in this acrimonious atmosphere the Church of England candidates withdrew 'en bloc', thus surrendering their traditional position as the majority. Mortimer was dismissed by the new Board, and his death six months later added emotional fuel to the fire. The process of replacing him led the Board into conflict with the National Union of Teachers. A boycott was placed on the school and the appointment of a new head, James Sydall, precipitated the mass resignation of the staff – one of the first national examples of direct action by teachers! Sydall was hounded out of office, a new head, Benjamin Crosby, was appointed and the furore died down. At the next election the Anglicans returned and resumed their majority compact with the Catholic members.

During the dispute Kate Ryley crossed pens with Charles Weld-Blundell, an opponent of board schools and an ardent supporter of denominational schools. He was scathing in his ridicule of her, declaring that he was confused by her:

> . . . incoherent lamentations, . . . which if carefully printed affords alike by its grammar and construction, abundant proofs of the incapacity of women for the discharge of the duties of public censorship.[21]

This was a rather odd indictment of a graduate of St. Andrew's, who was one of the first British women to receive a degree.

Following the Education Act of 1902 school boards were abolished and local authorities took on responsibility for education. Birkdale was not a borough, and responsibility for its schools passed to the Education Committee of the Lancashire County Council. The impact of the dramatic increase in the cost of this arrangement to Birkdale ratepayers has received scant recognition from local historians. In its last year the cost of the Birkdale School Board had been £1,750, a rate of 4d in the pound. The Lancashire Education Authority brought no new educational facilities to Birkdale, but the township had to share the cost of the rapidly expanding County Hall bureaucracy and provide cross-subsidy to other parts of the county with more pressing educational needs. In 1910 Birkdale contributed £9,000 to Lancashire, a rate of 1s 6d in the pound. The vastly increased cost of its education was an important factor in the financial crisis faced by Birkdale prior to amalgamation with Southport.

LEISURE AND RECREATION

In addition to their spiritual and educational roles, the chapels and churches contributed richly to the social and cultural life of east Birkdale. They sponsored a variety of groups and clubs. These included very active football, cricket, and tennis clubs. Perhaps the most famous Birkdale sportsman to emerge from this background was Jimmy Fay, whose boyhood home was at the Chatham Road end of Upper Aughton Road. An apprentice painter and a former pupil of St. Teresa's school, he played his early football and cricket for local teams. He went on to play football in the First Division of the English League for Bolton Wanderers, later becoming the first secretary of the Professional Footballers' Association. Following his success at football, he moved across the track to play his cricket for the fashionable Southport and Birkdale Club. A local sporting celebrity, he opened a successful sports outfitting shop in Southport. He later became a Justice of the Peace and, having a fine tenor voice, he frequently performed in concerts and with the local operatic society.

As well as the church clubs there were other unsectarian groups. In 1900 some fifteen local men banded together to form Birkdale Working Men's Club. They rented premises at 12 Kew Road, previously a hay and straw warehouse. Supported by local councillors, this non-political group flourished. The club, where no intoxicating drinks were served, provided a reading-room and a games-room. The landowner objected to this breach of the covenant of the lease and, despite widespread local support for the club, it was compulsorily closed. It appears that he later relented and the premises became Birkdale Men's Institute.

Kate Ryley founded Birkdale Working Lads' Club, which met in her Broome Road premises. As well as its very active social and sporting dimensions, this successful club provided opportunities for instruction in crafts. Girls were not neglected and she used the premises for meetings of the Birkdale Association for the Protection of Girls. Her sister Emily opened the Chatham Road Coffee Rooms. Another group sponsored by Kate, was a well-supported branch of the Anti-Smoking League. She was also closely involved in the provision of the Birkdale Recreational Evening Classes at the Board School.

An interesting development in east Birkdale was a special club for boy golf caddies. Caddying was a popular source of full-time employment for school leavers in Birkdale. Concern for the present and particularly the future welfare of these boys prompted Birkdale Golf Club to set up a Caddie Boys' Association in 1908.[22] As well as providing clothing and boots for the boys, generous backing from Club members allowed the Association to obtain a club-house at 51 Brighton Road. These premises, where smoking and gambling were forbidden, included games' rooms, a gymnasium, and facilities for the boys to have a bath. In addition to the leisure activities, the Association had an important commitment to find future employment for the boys, who were instructed in craft skills.

The call to the colours was also heard in Birkdale. In 1877 Captain Commander, later Lieutenant-Colonel, William Macfie formed a Birkdale detachment of the 13th Lancashire Rifle Volunteers, which met twice a week in rooms behind the Blundell Arms Hotel. Later, Thomas Weld-Blundell offered Macfie a site for a drill hall at 98 Upper Aughton Road. The company of 'Birkdalians' rapidly grew to over 100 strong and had its own drum and fife band, which frequently played in the township. This local detachment was lost when the Rifle Volunteers were absorbed into the Southport Volunteer Battalion of the King's Regiment. The Chatham Road Drum and Fife Band continued this local musical tradition.

There were also attempts to form brass bands in Birkdale. These included a short-lived Birkdale Town Band, whose instruments were passed on to the Brighton Road Methodist Men's Brotherhood Brass Band. It seems that Birkdale did not share the brass band traditions of inland Lancashire or, perhaps more significantly, the bands did not enjoy the industrial sponsorship available there. Nevertheless, a farm in Vaughan Road was the family home of William Rimmer, who was to become a distinguished brass bandmaster and composer, with a national reputation. It appears that William started his band career as a side drummer in Birkdale's Rifle Volunteers' Band.

A different but very successful musical venture was the formation of the Black Diamond Minstrels, who entertained at many of Birkdale's important events. Their secretary was W. Bradshaw of 63 Kew Road and the group rehearsed at Kate Ryley's Broome Road premises.

Following the demise of the Rifle Volunteers there was a different kind of music to be heard in the Drill Hall, when Messrs Davenport and Wood – "Caterers in the Terpsichorean Line" – held dancing classes. Later James Calling conducted his "Dancing Academy" at nearby 84 Upper Aughton Road. Many Birkdale residents acquired their ballroom dancing skills at this long-lasting establishment. The Drill Hall regained some of its martial associations as the headquarters of the Birkdale Company of the short-lived Baden Powell's Own Cadet Corps. The Corps failed because of opposition from the military, who were promoting Cadet Corps attached to their Volunteer Battalions. The Boy Scout movement superseded the Baden Powell Corps and Birkdale soon had its first troop, which included a cycle patrol and was attached to St. Peter's Church.

In 1912 a Picturedrome came to Birkdale when the Magistrates approved Mr. Schofield's plans for the "Picture Palace" to be built in Walton Road (now Mosley Street). Although the management intended to show religious films on Sundays, the application was opposed by St. Peter's, whose Sunday School stood directly opposite.

A glaring omission from east Birkdale's amenities was play facilities for the numerous children. Victoria Park was too far away and, moreover, unaccompanied children from "the other side of the line" were not welcomed. House building had left no open space suitable for a park between the railway and Chatham Road. In 1907 a partial solution was found. The Council leased a small plot alongside, and belonging to, the United Free Methodist Chapel. Although it was not big enough for playing ball games, the small recreation ground was fenced and furnished with swings and parallel bars. It became so popular that the Education Committee asked the Council to close it during school hours because of its adverse effect on children's attendance and punctuality. The request was refused. Stone throwing from this small playground repeatedly caused damage to the adjoining chapel and to the street light.

Later a more satisfactory park was developed further inland, on the site of the Birkdale Golf Club's original links. In 1909 the Council received six acres from Charles Weld-Blundell in settlement of an action concerning the foreshore (see Chapter Eight). The land, located between Bedford, Kew, Longford and Clifford Roads, was a wilderness of dunes. Plans were made which included a children's playgound, games areas, bowling greens, and a main walk linking the Lodge, in Bedford Road, to Clifford Road. A loan of £3,000 was obtained to pay for the development. Because of the cost involved, however, it was decided to leave much of the dune land to provide attractive natural walks. Work was well under way, providing employment for up to 80 unemployed labourers, when amalgamation came. It appears that Birkdale was considering using a second royal name – Alexandra – for the new park, which we now know as Bedford Park.

In the absence of conveniently sited recreation grounds the streets of New Birkdale served as playgrounds. A former Upper Aughton Road resident has given an account describing some of the games played by Birkdale youngsters. He recalls that: top and whip was popular, with the top being jammed upright between paving stones before it was first whipped; hop-scotch grids and numbers were marked on pavement tiles with a piece of soft brick or limestone; marbles were played up and down the gutter using cheap clay marbles or glass 'ollys'; skipping was a favourite with girls, old lengths of rope were cherished and numbers of children would skip in unison to the words of a skipping song or chant.

> Tag was a great game on cold days. Traps were set to catch the unwary, the less energetic or the less skilful. Leapfrog never lost its place in this catalogue of physical activities.[23]

MIDDLE-CLASS ESTATES EAST OF THE LINE

When Charles Weld-Blundell inherited Birkdale in 1887, his father had already sold the best building land in Birkdale Park to the Birkdale Park Land Company. It was for this reason that Charles looked to land which he still owned to the east of the railway line, for opportunities for middle-class development. In 1888 he repeated his father's strategy of offering land for a park to the Local Board, in an attempt to stimulate villa building. Unlike his father's earlier proposal, in which he had offered land in Birkdale Park, Charles was now offering a plot situated inland of the railway line:

> Sir – I propose to convey to the Local Board, for a free and open park for public recreation, a piece of land measuring nearly seven acres, situate between Liverpool Road and the Lancashire and Yorkshire Railway, opposite the Birkdale Cricket Club Ground. I am prepared to enclose the same with a substantial stone-coped wall, with railings on top, and to contribute 10,000 young trees for next Autumn planting, providing that the Board for their part undertake to lay it out and maintain the same in a suitable manner, and bear the cost of the railing and one half of the road making along the eastern border, and also erect a lodge and such gates as appear to be required for public convenience of access. I would suggest that the two principal entrances should be [i] on the Burlington-road, at the western side of the park, for the dwellers on the seaside of the line; [ii] on the Liverpool-road, at the eastern side, for the still larger population along that road and beyond.[24]

So anxious was Weld-Blundell to have the scheme adopted that his agent (Captain Simmonds) offered to take on the position of keeper without salary. Opponents of the scheme pointed to the implications for the rates. They noted that Birkdale was not a smoky manufacturing town where people never got pure air or saw a green field. They also had doubts about how effective this park would be in attracting additional quality houses and thus rate income. The offer was refused.

Tram in St. Peter's Road.

Stanley Avenue in 1909.

Growth inland, from the established middle-class area around Crosby Road and Welbeck Road, continued without the fillip to building which a park might have given. Eastbourne Road West (Crescent Road) was linked by a railway crossing to its continuation in Birkdale Park–Grosvenor Road. This proximity helped to enhance the status of the road, which was the site for a number of major villas. Development further along Liverpool Road was helped by the opening, in 1884, of Birkdale's second tramway, which linked the area with Southport, via St. Peter's Road and Everton Road. A principal beneficiary was Stanley Avenue. This was an interesting development, as the builders apparently ignored the Birkdale Local Board. No plans for Stanley Avenue had been approved, but inefficiency on the part of the local administration meant that it had no official bye-laws at the time, and, therefore, no action could be taken. The road was built narrower than the 36 feet which the Board had been allowing, and the front gardens were shorter. For many years Stanley Avenue was not adopted or cleansed by the local authority and was blocked at one end.

Coinciding with the departure of Birkdale Golf Club to its new links, Weld-Blundell started to develop a new estate behind Liverpool Road, the other boundaries being Brighton Road, Kew Road and Bedford Road. This "Dinorwic Estate" took its name from 'Dinorwic House', a substantial house, the extensive grounds of which were used in the development. The estate was to consist of Carlisle Road, which had been laid out earlier, but had been slow to build up, and three new roads. The Estate was proposing to call them Salisbury, Beaconsfield and Portland. At the request of the Council, Weld-Blundell agreed to the substitution of the names of two local political leaders – Barrett and Clinning – for those of the two national figures, whilst the name of the fourth road was changed from Portland to Dinorwic in deference to Southport, which already had a street bearing that name. Weld-Blundell was aiming for middle-class patronage.

The intention was not to build houses of the grandeur of Birkdale Park's "Castles in the Sand"; the estate was to consist of detached and semi-detached houses with a value of about £700 and a rental of between £35 and £45 per annum. Access to the estate was principally via Liverpool Road, with its tramway link with Southport. Seeking respectability through social seclusion, there was no road giving direct access to the working-class property in and beyond Kew Road. By 1899 50 houses had been built and the estate was the fastest growing part of the township. Many of the new houses were:

> erected on modern lines, dull red brick giving place to stucco work, and other materials offering variety . . . the design of the new premises shows that the monotonous squareness of rooms is obviated by means of bays and nooks. So much is this so that one rarely comes across a plan of the old type.[25]

Barrett Road.

The rich variety resulting from the work of these builders is still apparent.

Development had placed 'Dinorwic House', which had stood empty for a number of years, in Clinning Road. This fine older building was to acquire notoriety as "Birkdale's Haunted House". There had long been local legends of a ghostly presence in the sandhills. In 1901, with the approach of winter, it seems that the ghost seized its chance to abandon the open-air life and haunt in the indoor comfort of a spacious empty house. Stories of strange occurrences at 'Dinorwic House' spread rapidly. The Weld-Blundell Estate was naturally anxious to play down these accounts, as they could have an adverse effect not only on the letting of 'Dinorwic House', but also on the development of the new estate. A local reporter obtained the keys of the property by posing as a potential purchaser. He spent the night in the house and published a report claiming that he had heard peculiar noises and seen a ". . . wonderful ball of white light which revolved slowly along the floors."[26] This publicity had its effect. Each evening crowds of the curious assembled outside the house. Many arrived in cabs and stayed on late into the night. Bricks were thown at the house and damage done. As a result the Estate had the property guarded by its Watchers and special duty policemen. As ghost fever built up in Birkdale a gang of about 100 youths descended on 'Dinorwic House' and attacked it, breaking windows and roofing slates. Ironically they had just left their Sunday School. This act of vandalism led to a number of the boys appearing in court and being fined.

The court case added to the notoriety of "Birkdale's Haunted House" and it was investigated by the Psychic Research Society, which took evidence from the reporter who had witnessed the ghostly happenings. One local builder later claimed that his bankruptcy was a result of not being able to sell two houses which he had built opposite 'Dinorwic House'. He argued that the story of the ghost deterred potential buyers. Four years after the story broke, the journalist whose account of the ghostly goings-on had stimulated the hysteria wrote a letter to the *Southport Visiter* admitting that he had perpetrated a hoax which had got out of hand. The letter was discreetly tucked away, without editorial comment, in the Correspondence Column.[27] Despite this belated admission, the association of Clinning Road with "Birkdale's Haunted House" persisted, and many older residents still recall family tales of Birkdale's Ghost.

Charles Weld-Blundell was able to give a further boost to the promotion of this area when he accepted the Chairmanship of the local Council in 1902. He

Manor Lodge.

111

offered to build a library for the township in Liverpool Road. The site was on land he had reserved to build a manor house for himself. It was to adjoin 'Manor Lodge', between Stanley Avenue and Richmond Road. He had not abandoned his idea of a park in this area and envisaged such a development, including a museum, behind the proposed library. He had left the plot open, allowing public access, and had even furnished it with seats. This central plot could have become the hub of Weld-Blundell's greater Birkdale after Ainsdale was integrated. Significantly, the Estate Office was built in this area, at the corner of Stanley Avenue and Blundell Drive. Although the library did not materialise, house building continued.

This area also spawned a number of private schools to cater for the children of the neighbourhood. Middle-class families would not send their children to Birkdale's elementary schools, neither could they afford the fees of the superior private schools of Birkdale Park. In response to these market forces a number of small, relatively cheap, private day schools emerged. In Liverpool Road North Scarisbrick College accommodated 40 boys, with a further 30 at Birkdale Grammar School. There were, however, fewer cheap private schools for girls. It seems that many parents chose to send their daughters by the tramway to St. Andrew's Higher Grade School in Southport. This highly successful elementary school, which attracted girls from a very wide area, achieved much of its success at the expense of the cheaper private schools.

Perhaps the most famous scion of middle-class Birkdale east of the railway line, was the distinguished Oxford historian A.J.P. Taylor. The son of a cotton merchant, he was born in 1906 at a house in Barrett Road, and later lived at 18 Crosby Road. His account of his boyhood throws light on east Birkdale during these Edwardian years. He recollected:

> I went to a kindergarten, kept by Misses Filmer, two roads nearer the sandhills. I should remember the name if I heard it.[28]

His school was in fact Birkdale Preparatory School, at 22 Stanley Avenue. This was a small relatively cheap neighbourhood school catering for both girls and boys. The more expensive preparatory schools of Birkdale Park were exclusively for boys.

Taylor classified his family as wealthy migrants from industrial Lancashire. Their Crosby Road home was relatively large, with four or five bedrooms. His father travelled to work every day in Manchester, first catching the electric train from Birkdale to Southport. "He always wore a blue serge suit and a bowler hat. He smoked Havana cigars." Young Taylor's perception of his father's affluence would have been coloured by the context of the neighbourhood. For example, they had the only telephone in Crosby Road. By contrast, however, the majority of the residents living in the large houses on the other side of the

The Ainsbury family, Crosby Road, c. 1913.

railway in Birkdale Park were telephone subscribers. The Ainsbury family, near neighbours of the Taylors in Crosby Road, did run a two-seater Calthorpe car. Like so many residents in east Birkdale, the Taylors were active Nonconformists and Liberals regarding the Church of England as ". . . attended only by landlords and other wicked Tories." As a boy, A.J.P. attended the Sunday School of the Congregational Chapel, across the line in Grosvenor Road.

Robert Diggle Kay was another east Birkdale celebrity. When he died, in 1897, his widow had a stained glass memorial window installed in Wesley Methodist Church in Upper Aughton Road. The inscription described him as the originator and first publisher of the famous Bradshaw's Railway Guide, a claim which was vigorously contested by Bradshaw's family. Kay lived in Eastbourne Road West, now Crescent Road. A Nonconformist, he was also a Liberal and unsuccessfully fought a local election on their behalf.

It is interesting to note that during this era the majority of the township's politicians lived in this emerging middle-class area. The residents of Birkdale Park had discovered that they did not have to be councillors in order to exercise municipal power. In 1907, of the twelve councillors representing Birkdale wards seven lived inland of the railway, around Liverpool Road

CHAPTER SIX

A NEW TOWN CENTRE FOR BIRKDALE

Old Birkdale had been a township of scattered farms and cottages without a parish church or manor house to act as a focus. The railway station, with its road crossing and pedestrian subway, was the link between Birkdale Park and east Birkdale, and it was around the station that a town centre eventually developed. Most towns grow outwards from their town centre. New Birkdale had grown outwards from Southport as its southern suburb, and its own centre was only put in place later.

BIRKDALE'S MUNICIPAL BUILDINGS

In the minds of most old Birkdale residents, the symbol of Birkdale's independent existence was the block of municipal buildings in Weld Road. Its demolition, in 1971, and subsequent replacement with shops and flats has been much criticised. In fact its story is a commentary on the frugal attitude to public expenditure which consistently characterised Birkdale's administration.

Initially the Birkdale Local Board met in a room of a private school in York Road which was run by their clerk, Cyrus Johnson. This accommodation did not meet the civic aspirations of some of the early members of the Board and the question of a Town Hall was raised, but nothing was done. By 1870, the Board was meeting at Johnson's new school premises – 'Birkdale Lodge' in Lulworth Road. It was in this year that an agreement was negotiated with Thomas Weld-Blundell for a plot of land for a Town Hall at the corner of Weld Road and York Road, on the fringe of Birkdale Park.

Weld-Blundell insisted that the building should cost at least £2,000. Sensitive to the ratepayers' opposition to municipal extravagance, the Board chose to accept this minimum as their maximum; consequently the building was modest in concept, costing much less than many of Birkdale's villas. It was a symmetrical, brick built building, with a middle tower with a French-style hipped roof. There were offices either side of the entrance hall and the Board room running across the 30 foot length of the building at the rear. On the first floor was a large assembly room, which the Board regarded as an income generating asset. Unfortunately for the Board, the social cachet of holding events at the Palace or the Smedley Hotels proved a handicap to this ambition. The opening appears to have passed unmarked by celebration.

Charles Weld-Blundell marked his succession to the Estate, in 1887, with the gift of a three-dial illuminated clock for the tower. Several years later the question of adding a chiming bell was considered. The Board recognised that a bell would be a useful aid for timekeeping for poor residents living on the other side of the line, but decided that it would constitute a nuisance for the residents of Birkdale Park.

As Birkdale's municipal bureaucracy grew, the accommodation within the Town Hall proved increasingly inadequate. Maintenance and upkeep were neglected, the building was soon in a dilapidated condition and little income

Birkdale Town Hall and Police Station, c. 1900.

115

was generated. There were a number of abortive schemes to replace the Town Hall with a new building. In 1897 the Council eventually approved a compromise plan for a £3,600 extension, but although sanction for a loan was obtained, it was not built. In 1904 there was a further scheme for an extension costing £6,400, but this was the victim of the acute financial crisis which the Council was facing.

Birkdale's original Police Station and lock-up was located in Kent Road, inland of the railway. In 1880 Superintendent Jervis unsuccessfully sought the use of property behind the Town Hall for this purpose. There was also pressure to have a court in Birkdale, as Birkdale cases had to go to Southport. Critics suggested that the campaign was motivated by the vanity of some Birkdale Park residents who wanted to become magistrates. In 1884 a deputation from the Southport magistrates inspected Birkdale Town Hall and was impressed by the potential of the first-floor assembly room for a court, but the Board decided not to allow its use. It was left to the new Lancashire County Council, which took over responsibilities for policing, to come up with the money. In 1889 the County agreed to give £2,000 to erect a Petty Sessions Court. The Police Committee suggested that:

> . . . as Birkdale is a fashionable place, the residents might wish the building to be of a more expensive character than the bare necessities require. Perhaps the Board would offer a free site near the Town Hall and a sum of money for the embellishment of the building.[1]

The Birkdale Council already held the land around the Town Hall, and was thus able to offer a plot for a building to house the court, police station and cells. The members were not minded to accept the invitation to contribute to the cost in order to obtain a more elaborate building. As with the Town Hall, the opening was not marked by any celebration. Indeed, at the first sitting of the magistrates, in April 1892, the Chairman launched an extraordinary attack on the inadequacies of the building.

One of the features requested by the magistrates had been a mortuary – "The tide is continually leaving its dead on the broad and level sands of this coast."[2] Although omitted from the original plan, there was later a scheme for a mortuary costing £250, but nothing was done. The matter was brought to a head when the firemen objected to bodies being left in the fire station and the Council, which had to find the cost, eventually settled for a £30 chamber in the police yard.

Whatever the functional shortcomings of the buildings, the Board did spend some money on improving the frontage. The pavement was widened and boulevarded with tree planting. A new civic core to the Township, that had so lacked a centre, was developing.

The next addition to the emerging municipal complex was the Fire Station.

The Waterworks Company had earlier provided hydrants for fighting fires but the Birkdale Local Board had no apparatus to attach to them. In the case of fire, Birkdale residents had to cope as best they could, or wait for the arrival of the Southport Brigade. In 1863 a fire at Mr. Welsby's West Cliff Road home was out of control, and the house was almost completely gutted before the arrival of appliances from Southport. Some ten years later the Board got around to considering the possibility of a Birkdale brigade. A committee was set up and it reported that a cart and equipment could be bought for under £100, but nothing was done. When action finally came, in 1876, it was because the lack of a fire brigade had become an issue in Southport's campaign for incorporating Birkdale. A cart was obtained and a volunteer brigade of eight men raised.

The volunteers were paid a small retainer and a turn-out fee. The Board's parsimony was evident in the equipment provided for this force. Two years after its formation the volunteers had not been issued with helmets. The cart was kept at the Board's yard close to the station, whilst the majority of the volunteers lived on the Common, which was too distant for them to be able to hear the alarm bell. In an effort to increase efficiency, they were replaced by men from New Birkdale. Major reorganization did not come about until the end of the century, when a more professional regime of training was instituted and the brigade was provided with modern equipment. In 1900 a new fire station was built to the east of the police station in Weld Road. It was set back behind the line of the other municipal buildings, because the owners of the neighbouring building had been able to successfully claim that the original plan, to follow the building line, would have resulted in their light being blocked.

The fire brigade benefited from the Council's more liberal attitude towards borrowing and municipal expense, which was evident for a brief period around the turn of the century. The generous treatment of the fire brigade might not have been unconnected to the appointment, in 1898, of J.F. Keeley, the Board's Accountant, as its Captain. It was certainly his pride and joy, becoming the flagship of the authority. The brigade reached new levels of efficiency: the firemen had electric alarms fitted in their homes; Birkdale beat Southport to obtaining a new steam fire-engine; the brigade regularly took part in demonstrations; and they were paraded on every municipal occasion.

Attendance at the 1905 Hall Road railway disaster, in which over 20 people were killed, spurred Keeley to campaign for the provision of an ambulance van. In the absence of action from the Council, he launched an appeal and the cost was met by donations. A canvas-topped ambulance, embellished with Birkdale's coat-of-arms, was built by Walter Manning of Chatham Road. It was manned by members of the fire brigade, who had first-aid qualifications. As with the fire-engines, carriage-horses were provided by Goulders, whose stables were in the adjoining yard. Southport did not have an ambulance, and Birkdale was able to provide and charge it for this service.

Carnegie Library and Fire Brigade.

The final piece in the municipal jig-saw was the Public Library, which was built in the gap between the Town Hall and the Police Station in 1905. The Public Libraries Act of 1855 had enabled a local authority to raise a penny rate towards the running of a library, but this money could not be used to contribute towards the capital cost. The possibility of Birkdale having a public library was first mooted in the Board in 1877, the year in which William Atkinson donated £8,000 for a library and art gallery in Southport. Unfortunately no benefactor came forward in Birkdale. The reluctance of residents to contribute to local appeals was an unusual feature of the township. It appeared that many retained a strong allegiance to the towns in which their wealth had been generated, and there were numerous examples of Birkdale residents making generous gifts for civic, ecclesiastical and charitable purposes in other towns.

In 1887 the possibility of Birkdale celebrating the Queen's Jubilee with a library was considered, but apathy led to the scheme being dropped. Through the 1890s agitation again built up, stimulated, perhaps, by the knowledge that Southport had opened a branch library in Churchtown. The Council considered the possibility of using a room in the Town Hall or in the Board School, or of hiring a shop for a library, but it did not have the will to act. At the Diamond Jubilee of 1897 a subscription fund for a library was opened. The response was derisory and ". . . enthusiasm dwindled to nothingness." Discussing the provision of a library, a newspaper commentator observed that: ". . . the wealthier residents of West Ward who possess their own libraries, if they be persons of literary tastes, will have no use of it."[3] In fact the Park already had a private subscription library run by Mrs. Walker at 33 Weld Road, which offered the residents the newest publications.

Following the Queen's death, a further appeal was launched, but again the fund was slow to grow. As has been seen, the impasse appeared to have been broken when Charles Weld-Blundell decided to mark his Coronation Year chairmanship of the Council with the gift of a plot of land for a library, along with £1,000 for the building. It was to be known as the Weld-Blundell Library but was to be built in Liverpool Road, between Stanley Avenue and Richmond Road. The strength of local opposition to a free library, with its subsequent charge on the rates, was evident when a deputation of wealthier ratepayers attended a Council meeting in order to object.

Nevertheless, the scheme went forward. The plot had been levelled and pegged out, when Birkdale's long-running library saga took another extraordinary turn. The Council followed the example of many other towns and appealed to Andrew Carnegie, the wealthy steel magnate and philanthropist, for help. (Carnegie supported the building of nearly 3,000 libraries.) The response was immediate – Birkdale was given a grant of £5,000. Weld-Blundell welcomed this development, suggesting that the Carnegie Library should be built alongside the Town Hall, while his library could be built in Shaftesbury Road, to serve the Common.

In a competition to design the Carnegie Library, the £50 prize was won by George Brown, an architect living in Dover Road. The building included a lending department, to hold 10,000 volumes and a reading room. Probably its most striking feature was the large entrance hall, clad in glazed bottle-green tiles. On the walls were two handsome mosaic tablets acknowledging the benefactors. A smaller beaten copper plaque listed the members of the Library Committee.

The extent of the Council's financial problems was revealed when it considered the question of the pavement outside the library. There was a prolonged debate and a split vote before it was decided to lay flags at a cost of £19, rather than asphalt costing only £9. The need for economy was also evident in an attempt to buy second-hand library books from Manchester and Liverpool.

The Library was opened in 1905 by Hall Caine, an author who had previously lived in Birkdale. It was estimated that the ceremony was attended by over 1000 residents. It was the first time that Birkdale had celebrated a civic event in such style. Egerton Castle and William Watson, two other authors with local connections, were approached and asked to donate books. Watson, a poet, was much offended by this invitation and wrote a letter headed "Literature and Lucre" to the *Daily News*. He suggested that the Council had been generously treated by Carnegie, and criticised it for soliciting books ". . . free gratis and for nothing". He went on to accuse Birkdale of ". . . fantastic parsimony".[4] The parsimony did not prevent the newly image-conscious Council from producing an attractive plate for its books. Despite the lack of ambition and resolve on the part of Birkdale's administrators, the Township finally had a set of municipal buildings easily accessible from both sides of the railway line.

SHOPPING AND COMMERCIAL CENTRE

As Birkdale Park had initially come into being as a suburb of Southport, residents had largely used Southport for shopping. It appears to have been the middle-class development east of the line which led to the emergence of a conveniently situated shopping centre in Liverpool Road. The initiative came from Joseph Mather who lived in this area. In 1894, he built a line of four new shops, and these were quickly occupied. From Southport's Lord Street came Henry Hayes, a wine and spirit merchant; E. Robinson, also of Lord Street, opened a fish and game shop; Leigh's the butchers has served Birkdale for many years and happily much of the shop's original interior has been retained; whilst Mrs. Blaylock's shop sold stationery, fancy goods and included a subscription library. Banks were attracted to this evolving centre by the prosperity of Birkdale's residents. In 1894 two cottages (numbers 1 and 3) were demolished to accommodate a branch of the Manchester and Salford Bank, which had shared premises with a chemist for the previous six years, and soon there were four other banks on Liverpool Road. The road was widened and straightened. Councillor E.A. Hodge was the builder of further shops, and over a period of time the front gardens of the older properties were surrendered to the Council in order to give broad pavements, which were enhanced by the addition of verandahs and tree planting. Charles Weld-Blundell visited the development in 1906 and was very impressed, particularly by the trees which were meeting overhead.

He must also have been impressed with the range and quality of the shops. On the north side, the quaint isolated building alongside the railway track was the premises of William Culshaw, a motor engineer. Richard Bamber, the cycle manufacturer, had also opened a garage and workshop further inland. There was just one shop west of Alma Road, that of Thomas Fell, a stationer and tobacconist, who also ran a circulating library. Between Alma Road and Bolton Road was a block of shops. The large Alma Road corner site was occupied by Hiscock's, a grocer and provision merchant. Adjoining this were Thomas Unsworth's premises. He was a baker and confectioner, whose claimed

Shops on the south side of Liverpool Road.

Shops on the north side of Liverpool Road.

speciality was "bridescake", and alongside his shop he had a cafe to provide refreshment for shoppers. Next, on the site of the Midland Bank, came Frank Street, a cabinet maker and house furnisher. This was followed by Gibson and Kendrew, ironmongers, Ernest Fennell's fish, game and poultry shop, Bamber's premises and petrol pump, J.C. Thurgarland, a boot and shoemaker, and John Coward, a hairdresser and umbrella seller. On the south side there was Burgon's grocery and provision shop, Leigh's the butcher, Mrs. Ellen Turner, a confectioner, Charles Hare, a druggist and chemist, who was also a councillor, Henry Hayes' wine and spirit shop, Mrs. Jane Ingham, a draper, John Kellit, a grocer, and Mrs. Robinson a licensed game merchant who also sold fruit. This commercial development complemented the administrative buildings and belatedly provided Birkdale with its own town centre.

SOCIAL AND POLITICAL AMENITIES

One of the earliest buildings in this "town centre" area was the Park Hotel, built in 1859. Standing in Weld Road, between Birkdale Park and east Birkdale, it was used until 1874 for meetings of the Leet Court, through which Weld-Blundell was able to direct tenants to undertake such functions as clearing ditches and watercourses. Failure to attend the court led to the imposition of a fine. Before an Estate Office was opened, Weld-Blundell's agent also used the Park Hotel, which adjoined the railway station, to meet potential Birkdale Park residents. Prior to the Town Hall being built, the Local Board considered using rooms at the Park for its meetings and as its office.

It seems that the Park Hotel was not very fashionable. There were frequent complaints about rowdy behaviour in its vicinity. The clientele was mainly drawn from the other side of the line (bowling tournaments and exhibition matches attracted large crowds). Possibly more attractive to residents of Birkdale Park was the initiative displayed by Mrs. Sawyer, the proprietrix, in winter. When hard frost rendered the green unfit for play, she used one of her patent sprinkling machines to flood it in order to create a skating rink. This proved to be so popular that electrical lighting was installed.

The two major political parties each had a clubhouse in Liverpool Road. In 1889 Birkdale's Conservative Club moved from Everton Road to new premises on the site of two demolished cottages – numbers 6 and 8 Liverpool Road. The handsome building provided a range of social facilities for the members, including a reading room, two billiard rooms, a smoking room and bar. The Club still use the first floor rooms, and the crests in the stained glass windows on the staircase act as a reminder of Birkdale's history. Immediately behind the clubrooms the members were able to enjoy a game of bowls on the Club's own green. Birkdale's Liberal Club moved to a clubhouse at the corner of Liverpool

Road and Bolton Road in 1894 (now used by the Labour Party). Unlike the Conservative Club, alchohol was not served: in the words of the Club chairman, it was ". . . not a convenience for thirst."[5] This neglected clubroom was used as a talking-shop, where national issues were earnestly debated, rather than as a headquarters for local Liberal activists. When the Club later received a financial windfall from a Liberal bazaar held in Southport, it was eventually decided to spend the money on re-building and re-furbishing these rather dilapidated premises. This work included the addition of the corner tower, long to be a feature. A plaster sign beneath the tower proclaimed the purpose of the building.

By the time Birkdale amalgamated with Southport, it had a town centre which helped to preserve a sense of Birkdale's identity long after its administrative independence had gone. Now cherished by conservationists, the area has come to be known as "Birkdale Village".

CHAPTER SEVEN

THE COMMON: OLD BIRKDALE LIVES ON

I thought the roads in Birkdale were neglected but when I arrived at the famous "Common", I stood aghast, as I found all along the main road (Liverpool Road), there is not a safe footpath to walk upon, so that some hundreds of the resident population are forced into the heavy trafficked (sic) cart road. But at Halsall Road the conditions eclipsed everything I had seen. The asphalt in front of a little shop was smashed up and there were holes big enough for a dog to lay in. The footpath was strewn with ash pit refuse.

Liverpool Porcupine, October 1888

A LIVING FROM THE LAND

Birkdale Common was detached and distant from New Birkdale and initially little influenced by it. The Rev. Swift's daughter wrote that those not living on the Common were called "furreners" and so treated.[1] The census of 1851 shows us that, at the beginning of our period, over 80% of the male heads of household worked in farming. Sylvia Harrop, in *Old Birkdale and Ainsdale*, has already provided a detailed analysis of how distinctive patterns of husbandry evolved in Birkdale, where blown sand meets moss land. Rabbits were farmed on the warrens of the 'hawes', the local name for the sandy dunes. Arable land was cultivated and pastures grazed on the 'heys', where humus transformed the top layers of yellow sand into soil, whilst the damp low-lying peaty earth of the moss, inland of the township, yielded rich crops once drained. The 1861 census returns show that the suburban transformation in New Birkdale had made little impact on the Common. Some 78% of male householders were working in farming, and ten years later the figure was still 70% . A government report of 1873 referred to the Common as being ". . . almost wholly agricultural".[2] Few "furreners" had come to live on the Common: approximately threequarters of the householders had been born in Birkdale, and most of the others came from adjoining townships.

The Heys

Even before the development of New Birkdale, a growing local market for agricultural produce already existed with the nineteenth century development of Southport. Access to the markets of Liverpool was more difficult. Catherine Jacson, in her *Formby Reminiscences*, tells how the tall dunes formed an impenetrable barrier for a coastal road, whilst shortly after inheriting his estate, Thomas Weld-Blundell described the roads of south-west Lancashire as execrable. Taking their produce to market in Liverpool involved Birkdale farmers in a long cart journey over the circuitous inland route, through Halsall and Lydiate – a journey starting at four o'clock in the morning. A dramatic change came with the opening of the Liverpool, Crosby and Southport Railway. It was a boon to local farmers and, before succeeding as a commuter line, it had become known as the "Farmers' Line". Quick to recognise its importance, ". . . most farmers who were in a position to take shares took as many £5 shares as they could spare money for."[3]

The railway carried fresh milk into the city. Early morning loading of milk churns and field produce at Lloyd's Sidings, near the old Birkdale Station, became a daily routine. Liverpool also generated an enormous demand for animal feed and straw. In 1890 there were some 16,000 horses moving millions of tons of goods around the city. The railway was able to transport vast quantities of the manure created by these beasts, along with the night-soil of the citizens. Thousands of tons arrived annually at Lloyd's Sidings and were used to enrich the thin soil of Birkdale and thus increase both yields and the intensity with which the land could be farmed. As early as 1849 a writer in the *Liverpool Mercury* observed that: "The railway has brought fertility to the fields and the fields within reach of the market." Previously the manure had been carted from the Leeds and Liverpool Canal at Halsall.

Early in the nineteenth century Charles Blundell had acted to reduce the length of farming leases. This policy was continued by Thomas Weld-Blundell, who issued ever shorter leases. Granting short leases allowed him not only to increase his influence on how his land was farmed but also, at a time of rapid urban development in Birkdale, it gave the landowner the flexibility to use farm land for other purposes.

Thomas Weld-Blundell also continued the policy of keeping the farms small. Although costing more for buildings, small farms provided more rent than large farms. Additionally they could be looked after largely by members of the family. This normally meant that they were better kept. In 1851 the average size of the 25 Birkdale farms was 26 acres. On the largest, six men were employed farming 80 acres. By 1881 there were still sixteen separate farms on the Common, with seven of them under ten acres, and three of over 60, whilst the average size was 25 acres. Eight of the farms had Marshalls as tenants. They were one of Birkdale's largest families and had many branches. Other names included Aughton, Rimmer and Lloyd. The detailed stories of some of these

Jack Sawyer, a Birkdalian son of the soil.

farms and the families who farmed them is told in *Families and Cottages of Old Birkdale and Ainsdale* edited by Sylvia Harrop.

In building their characteristic low-slung cottages, the early inhabitants had to make the best of the paucity of local building materials. The framework was based on the mediaeval "cruck" form of construction. At each end of the cottage a cruck was formed by a bent or split tree trunk in the shape of an inverted 'V'. Longer buildings had additional crucks to give support. The rough-hewn timbers were secured by wooden pegs. One source of timber was the foreshore, with its harvest of driftwood. In the absence of local stone or clay for brick making, the walls were made by plastering daub on a rough lattice of wooden posts (clamstaff). The daub was made from a mixture of mud and chopped starr grass, stiffened by horse hair and cow dung. Charles Weld-Blundell referred to these cottages as "mud-stick-and-daub" buildings which, he argued, were easily made by the labourers themselves:

> . . . each taking turns to help his fellows making or repairing these simple structures, without any expense to the landowner beyond the rough hewn rafters and beams of support and the reeds, rushes or straw grown in their croft.[4]

126

The eaves of the smaller cottages were only five feet high, which governed the size of the leather-hinged doors. Windows were few and small, partially the residual effect of an earlier window tax, but also a response to the strong westerly winds. The interiors were limewashed, but local photographs reveal evidence of wall paintings being used as a form of decoration. Floors were paved with sanded flagstones, which had to be carted to the area. Deep thatch on the roofs provided superb all-the-year-round insulation – warm in winter and cool in summer. A small buttery, with a stone shelf for food storage, was normally found at the shaded north end of a cottage. The 1869 *General Rate Book* shows that the rentals for the majority of the cottages varied between £4 and £8, with the average being just under £6. These cottages were the cheapest dwellings in the township.

By 1851 some farm walls had been clad in brick and roofs slated. Many early cottages had only a 'shelf'-like second storey to provide sleeping spaces, with access gained by a small ladder. Some farms were built with a full second storey, or had one added. As a condition of their leases some tenants had to limewash their farms annually, and were responsible for repairing the buildings, fences and gates. The Estate took action against those who allowed farms to get into a dilapidated condition.[5]

Fields in Birkdale were known as 'heys' – the old English word for enclosure. The fields were enclosed by cops of earth up to five feet high. In addition to acting as field boundaries, cops also protected the light sandy soils from being carried away by the strong south-westerly winds. Trees were not indigenous to the area and it is interesting to note that local leases included the requirement to plant trees and hawthorn hedges. The results of this policy can be seen in contemporary photographs of Birkdale farms. Copses of trees provided shelter for the buildings and orchards; whilst hedge planting on the cops increased their effectiveness as wind breaks and provided cover for the abundant blackberry brambles. Several farms had a duck pond, and hens were always to be seen scratching around the yard.

Shippons for cows were a common feature on Birkdale farms, with many of the farmers keeping a small herd to produce dairy products for selling, rather than an individual cow to meet a family's own needs. In 1897 there were still some 157 cows in the township, producing over 600 gallons of milk daily. The occupations of "cowkeeper", "cowboy", and "dairymaid" all appear in the census returns. A number of the shippons fell short of local health requirements and the farmers were slow to replace them. An even greater hazard to health were the middens. In many cases these were located within a yard of the shippon doors, and in the absence of any drains to the sewers they were surrounded by a lake of urine. Such foul ponds were not only unpleasant, they posed a threat to the nearby shallow wells from which the drinking water for the cows was drawn. Sheep and the ubiquitous pigs were also kept. As the

Underhill Farm, near Windy Harbour Road.

population of Birkdale grew, so did the number of animals being fattened for slaughter. There had long been a pinfold, for the pounding of strays, at the heart of the old Common. As late as 1893, the Council ordered the sale of an unclaimed goat which had been held in the pinfold.[6]

There was a great variation in the quality of the soil in Birkdale. The land belonging to farms was not always confined to fields immediately adjoining them. As Sylvia Harrop has demonstrated in *Old Birkdale and Ainsdale*, there was a system by which good land was shared out. The richest soil was on the Gorstile – strips of land running down to the inland Boundary Brook. Indeed, several Birkdale farmers also held fields of rich damp peat land on Birkdale Moss, on the other side of this brook.

Arable farming on Birkdale's small farms had traditionally consisted of labour-intensive husbandry, with the growing of crops such as peas, beans, cabbages, potatoes, carrots, turnips and a local speciality – celery. "Celery Bob Rimmer" had a farm on the Gorstile near Halsall Road. Cereal crops were also grown, particularly on the larger farms. Evidence of the adoption of modern innovations is found in the village school log-book. In 1875, three boys lost their attendance marks through loitering on their way to school watching a couple of steam threshing-machines. The annual appearance of these Leviathans must have caused considerable local excitement.

During the nineteenth century, Birkdale farmers moved away from the tradition of keeping resident farm servants. Although they received a lower

Thatched cottage, Sandon Road.

wage than day labourers, the cost of providing their keep made them more expensive. Day labourers received between 15 shillings and £1 a week and the farmer also had to provide accommodation for them. Four-roomed cottages at 7 and 9 Sandon Road provide good examples. These were built in 1869. The local custom appears to have been for farmers to supply their tenants with a one-acre plot, with their cottage. Most of the labourers kept pigs on these smallholdings, and the master of the village school confirmed that: "Many of the cottagers are possessed of a cow, which requires the attention of a boy or girl to mind it while grazing." Any surplus produce from these smallholdings was sold to supplement the family income.

Birkdale Common women, described by the Rev. Swift's daughter as wearing ". . . a linsey wolsey skirt and a kind of bodice very simply made and a shawl",[7] would have travelled from Birkdale Station, with their large shallow baskets laden with homemade butter and cheese, to stand Liverpool market. On the farms women helped with harvesting, as did the children.

An interesting commentary on Birkdale's farming year is found in the comments made by the master of the village school in his Log Book, to explain the absence of many of the children during 1873.[8] The tasks undertaken by the children were mostly those where nimble fingers rather than strength were an asset.

April 28   Most of the older boys absent from school planting potatoes.

May 1   Only eight scholars present in standards III to VI. Those who are absent are engaged in outdoor labour.

June 2   Some of the boys in the upper classes absent weeding.

August 1   Many who have been at school this week absent today getting peas for tomorrow's market.

Sept. 29   Many of the older boys and girls absent from school today, cause of absence potato getting.

There was no mill on the Common and, although there had been a Birkdale Mill close to the boundary with Southport since the eighteenth century, the older Ainsdale Mill was more conveniently situated for the farmers of the Common. Thomas Rimmer, an 18-year-old, was the miller at Birkdale Mill in 1851, whilst his father William was the blacksmith. The presence of so many working horses on the Common probably persuaded John Makinson, a 30-year-old master blacksmith from Scarisbrick to move to Birkdale in 1853. His workshop was behind his cottage in Liverpool Road. In 1881 he was assisted by four of his sons. A fifth son worked in the family wheelwright's shop. Wagons for the farms were produced locally and there was a second wheelwright's shop, run from before 1851 by the Brookfield family, in the barn of South End Farm. The farmers' pub was the Crown, and in 1888 a double weighing machine was installed there for them. No doubt when they called to use it the opportunity was taken to slake their thirst.

The Hawes
The Mat Weavers: A Unique Cottage Industry
Birkdale had an unusual cottage industry – mat weaving from starr grass. The proceeds supplemented the incomes of many of the agricultural families. 'Starr' was the local name for the marram grass which grew in great abundance on the hawes. Starr is indigenous to the outer dunes and its long penetrating roots serve to bind the sand. It helps to stabilise the dunes, and thus protect inland areas from blown sand and inundation by the sea. The crucial importance of starr grass had long been recognised by the landowners, who used the law to protect it and thus their estates. Some of the local leases included the requirement for the tenant to plant starr, and the Estate accounts regularly showed payments for the employment of men planting starr.

The grass also had other properties. Its broad tough leaves could be dried to provide a material which the villagers had long used to weave mats, hats and baskets. The table-mats, similar to those now imported from Third World countries, were sometimes referred to as "knife and fork mats". Early in the nineteenth century, Glazebrook suggested that "a considerable quantity" of the grass was being "surreptitiously and clandestinely cut". He went on to caution the collectors to take care and avoid damaging the roots of the plant.[9] He recognised how vulnerable these friable dunes were to trampling.

In 1851 table-mat weaving was an important aspect of rural Birkdale's economy. It seems likely that the growth of Southport as a seaside resort helped to create a demand for these local craft products. Although there was only one male head of household who claimed this as his occupation, about a third of the households in the Township had at least one female working to supplement the family income in this manner. These females were aged anything between six and 80 years. Four were single or widowed heads of households, and almost all of the others were wives or daughters of agricultural labourers. On one small seven-acre farm all five daughters were table-mat makers, although four of them were of school age. That the mat-weavers were not afraid to declare their occupation to the census enumerator suggests that the law, which made even possession of starr an offence, was not being enforced.

The growth of Birkdale Park brought a new imperative to the question of protecting the outer sandhills, and Thomas Weld-Blundell was to change the previously relaxed approach. New notice boards forbidding the residents to take starr had little effect. Individual warnings were also ignored and, consequently, prosecutions were taken out. In July of 1854, William Rimmer was fined 6s 6d costs by the Southport Magistrates. The Estate thought this too lenient and its solicitor wrote to the magistrates' clerk pointing out the requirements of the law in respect to this offence. He replied that this being a first offence, the magistrates believed the punishment awarded would answer the purpose.[10] Further cases were brought in July 1857 when Peter Wright, a labourer, was charged with illegal possession of starr within five miles of the sandhills. Similar charges were made against five young children, one of them, Thomas Bond, being only ten. John Pye, the steward, explained to the magistrates that notices previously served against the defendants had been ignored. He reported that boards warning people who took starr that they would be prosecuted had been destroyed as soon as they were placed. Weld-Blundell's solicitor argued that the Estate was concerned for the preservation of the dunes and had reluctantly been forced to this extreme measure, having exhausted every other means.[11] This change of policy on the part of the Estate must have been perceived as a grievous attack on what the residents of the Common had come to regard as a right. Mr.

Gascoigne, a Birkdale Park 'Frontager', asked the magistrates for "lenient consideration" of the defendants, as "the working up of this starr" afforded employment to a great many families who might otherwise be thrown upon the parish. Wright was found guilty, but the magistrates were reluctant to impose the maximum sentence of three months in a "House of Correction" in a case where "the rights of the Lord of the Manor, though indisputable, had been allowed to remain in abeyance." He was fined £1 plus costs. The charges against the children were to be withdrawn on payment of expenses, and on condition that the parents and children signed a declaration to respect starr in future. Initially the parents refused to do so, but when the alternatives were explained to them they all signed. The following month a poster was issued, giving final notice that the laws relating to the illegal collecting of starr would be rigidly enforced. To reinforce this message a postscript gave the names and sentences passed on the six who had been recently prosecuted.

At the census four years after the court case only three residents declared their occupation as mat-weaver. They were: Jenny Roberts, a 55-year-old widow, her 17-year-old daughter, and Janet Watkinson, a 21-year-old spinster. Perhaps this was the situation in 1861, but ten years later, at the census in 1871, some 54 mat-weavers were listed. All female, the majority were the wives and daughters of agricultural labourers, although there were as many as seven women who were the head of household. At a sale-of-work held in the village school in 1872 women from the Common were offering mats for sale and the members of St. James', who had driven over from Birkdale Park to support their school, were buying them.

The most significant change shown in the 1871 census from that in 1851 was the absence of children recorded as mat-weavers. Schooling was not yet compulsory but, as will be seen later, the village school was having a bigger impact in the community. Only four mat-weavers under the age of 16 were listed, the youngest being 11. Although it was no longer a full-time occupation for children of the Common, they were still involved with starr grass. In an attempt to explain widespread absence from the village school in March 1872, the headmaster noted that ". . . nearly all the children engaged planting starr grass on the sand hills for Weld-Blundell Esq." Despite this legal and financially rewarding work they had not foresaken their old ways. In the following June, the headmaster recorded:

> The attendance is very poor . . . nearly all the absentees being engaged cutting and bleaching 'starrgrass' in the sandhills. This occupation prevents many children from attending school for six or seven weeks.

The last reference to the grass in the school log book occurred in 1875, when several children were recorded as being absent ". . . binding and crossing starr mats".

From about this time Weld-Blundell's agent employed ". . . a detective every summer to prevent the cutting of starr grass and to prosecute those who persisted."[12] Nevertheless, mat-weaving was still an economically important, if illegal, activity. A contemporary estimated that it was possible for a good weaver to earn as much as 12 shillings a week, approximately two-thirds of the wage of a day labourer. The 1881 census shows eighteen women and girls from the Common who were prepared to tell the enumerator that they were mat-makers. The illegal cutting of starr grass continued throughout the 1880s and prosecutions, though not numerous, occurred in most years.

Mat-weaving became a major issue in the first election for the new Lancashire County Council in 1889. Charles Weld-Blundell was the Liberal candidate and his opponent alleged that he was responsible for the stringent enforcement of the law, thus preventing local families from supplementing their income. After losing the election, Weld-Blundell reconsidered the matter and gave new instructions to his agent. Captain Simmonds addressed mat-weavers who had been summoned to a meeting in a field off Sandon Road. Despite wretched weather there was a large turn-out, and Simmonds told them that Weld-Blundell was prepared to license bona-fide local mat-weavers. They would have to register at the Birkdale Estate Office, giving their names and addresses, and would be issued with a ticket which would allow them to cut sufficient grass for their business, in the proper season and under the superintendence of one of the Estate's 'starr-watchers'. No other persons were to be allowed to cut grass, and Simmonds informed them that anybody else who was caught illegally collecting grass would be subject to the utmost rigour of the law. The crowd were well pleased with this offer and sang "For he's a jolly good fellow" as the agent drove off in his carriage.[13] The system appears to have worked satisfactorily, and prosecutions of mat-weavers dried up. Richard Crook, the 'starr-watcher', was kept busy protecting the dunes from a new nuisance, bringing actions against local builders who disturbed the grass in their illegal taking of sand.

In 1891 only three residents registered their occupation as mat-makers. They were Alice Leatherbarrow, a 78-year-old widow living at 21 Shaftesbury Avenue, her 46-year-old daughter, and another widow, 60-year-old Jane Marshall of Lloyd's Sidings. All three of them had been born in Birkdale. Although it will be some years before the 100-year rule allows inspection of the 1901 census, J. Carr, the Registrar of Birkdale who acted as chief enumerator, did divulge at the time that this cottage industry, which had occupied such a large percentage of Birkdale's cottagers in 1871, appeared to have totally disappeared by 1901. Although no longer an occupation, this unique local craft was handed down through Birkdale families and 'amateur' practitioners persisted.

As has been clearly demonstrated here Bailey, the major historian of Southport, was mistaken in his view that following the 1857 prosecution the villagers foresook the making of mats from starr grass in favour of basket-weaving from locally abundant willow. Evidence to support his view concerning basket-making from willow in Birkdale is also sparse. In 1881 there was only one resident, John Shipside of Stamford Road, who claimed this as his occupation. More colourfully, there is evidence involving gypsies. In 1859 there was an appearance at Southport Petty Sessions by the "chief of the tribe" camping in the neighbourhood of the Ash Tree Public House. He was seeking an extension to a notice to quit issued by the police. It was reported that the gypsies were reaping a rich harvest in fortune-telling, whereas their chief claimed that they had come for trading purposes and were honest and respectable. He supported his assertions by claiming that they had purchased large quantities of willow. In giving his evidence he had the support of one local resident – the landlord of the Ash Tree! In 1881, the census enumerator recorded that there was one gypsy family present in the township – 41-year-old Joshua Gray, his wife, their six children, and a further four nieces and nephews. They were all living in a tent alongside the Ash Tree, which had deteriorated into a state of complete dilapidation. The wife was described as a basket-maker. Twelve years later, William Brewer, a basket-maker, was fined 5 shillings for being a pedlar of wicker chairs without a licence.

Rabbit Warrens: Farming and Poaching

The sandy 'hawes' were also the location of Birkdale's extensive rabbit warrens. The dunes provided an ideal habitat for rabbits, particularly the inner more mature dunes, where other grasses had joined the starr to give a denser vegetation cover. The deep soft sand was ideal for burrowing, whilst on this marginal land the rabbits did not have to share the grazing with other animals. They were systematically farmed, but needed little attention. Nature ensured a plentiful supply, with rabbits breeding several times each season and producing up to eight young in each litter. Charles Weld-Blundell believed them to have the potential to become a major source of meat for the English working classes:

> No known animal, when properly treated and suitably fed, produces so much food in exchange for trifling and almost valueless diet, or yields a more useful fur. In truth, an ideal labouring man's food and by a strange accident there is nothing he likes as well.[14]

In 1900, after some of the Birkdale warrens had been lost to other purposes, it was said that they were still producing over 1000 rabbits a week.

Illegally taking rabbits proved to be a perpetual temptation for small-time local poachers. They were frequently detained and prosecuted by Weld-Blundell's 'watchers'. Rabbits being principally nocturnal creatures, poaching usually occurred under the cover of darkness. The customary defence offered in court was that the accused were picking mushrooms. Fines of 5s 0d or 10s 0d were the normal outcome. The motive for trespass on the warrens was not only commercial. The locals coursed rabbits with fox-terriers. In 1886, Weld-Blundell's agent denounced this practice as being cruel in the extreme. He claimed that it was ". . . upheld chiefly by the lowest class of betting men and poachers."[15] Ten years later local gamblers were still gathering in the seclusion of the warrens to play cards and pitch and toss. Following up complaints from Gilbert Marshall, the tenant of 'Rabbit Warren Farm', Richard Crook, Weld-Blundell's watcher, disturbed a group of over 30 men during one of their regular Sunday afternoon sessions. As on a previous occasion all but one – Shields – fled. He stayed to pick up the cards and the money. Challenged by Crook he "bunted" him under the chin with his head, knocking two teeth out, and then continued punching him after he fell.[16] It is interesting to note that Shields was successfully charged with trampling and damaging the starr grass, but not with assaulting Crook!

In the lease to Birkdale Golf Club, Weld-Blundell had reserved his rights to game. The question was, were rabbits game? Fortunately for the golf club they were deemed vermin and it was able to launch a major extermination drive. The club employed trappers, who used tarred sticks and sealed the burrows. The trappers succeeded, and dramatically reduced the number of rabbits on the links. There were no objections from the landowner; golf and the associated housing were more profitable uses of sand dunes than rabbit warrens.

SERVICES AND AMENITIES FOR THE COMMON

Under the old farmer-dominated Highway Board, more money was spent on roads on the Common than in Birkdale Park. After the setting-up of the Local Board, this state of affairs was reversed and more was spent in New Birkdale, although the cost of providing services on the Common still exceeded the rate income generated there. In addition to contributing relatively little to the township's rates, Birkdale Common presented major physical problems for the Local Board. There was a considerable distance between New Birkdale and the Common, whilst the scattered nature of the settlement meant that it was expensive to link it to the new services – gas, piped water, and sewerage. Not surprisingly the Common had the last call on these amenities.

Gas, which had been available in New Birkdale from the early 1860s, was not to reach the Common for over 20 years. There was a similar situation with piped water. Many residents were still dependent upon the shallow wells into the 1880s, despite tests revealing that the water was unfit for domestic use. By the 1890s much of the Common was receiving town water. It was, however,

1897 before Lloyd's Sidings, where there was a row of eighteen small cottages built for railway workers, was finally linked up.

Previously these densely populated houses had depended on:

> . . . two subsoil wells constructed of bricks with wood coverings. A small tin drum fastened on to a ladle seven feet long is plunged into the wells, water is thus drawn and siphoned into other vessels and carried to the dwellings forty yards away and used as required . . . Ashpits with privies attached are situate forty yards from these subsoil wells. There is no drainage to the property, waste water is thrown on the land and dug into some, chiefly for vegetable growing.[17]

Not surprisingly, as a result of drinking polluted well water, the residents had been subject to repeated outbreaks of fever. After much prevarication the Estate eventually agreed to connect Lloyd's Sidings to town water. These houses were still without gas at the end of our period. The linking of the Common to the main sewer was similarly delayed and it took much longer to complete the network. As late as 1892 Fredrick Burgh, of 85 Liverpool Road South, was complaining to the Board about the urgent need of sewers in Liverpool Road South, near Halsall Road, for about twenty cottages. Apparently sewage was running over the land, close to the houses, conditions exacerbated by the waste from the cows and pigs kept by many of the cottagers.

Under an Act of 1880, the new Southport and Birkdale Tramway Company was given power to run a line linking the Common with Southport. The terminus should have been at the Crown Hotel. When the line was finally opened in 1884, the financially hard-pressed Company had not fulfilled its commitments and the line terminated at Brighton Road, thus serving the more profitable new middle-class estates, but not the Common. The Company did undertake to provide a cheap omnibus link to the Crown Hotel. This service proved to be sketchy and unreliable. If Southport workers were to live on the Common, they needed early and late trams, which were not provided. When the Company was eventually forced to extend the line, it sometimes failed to provide the two trams scheduled to run to the Crown each day, because the receipts did not pay the wages of the workers.

Another cause of complaint was the manner in which the police were said to neglect the Common. A letter to the Board in 1878 claimed that there was never a policeman to be seen on the Common, whilst the scenes that were occurring there day after day were a disgrace to any civilised country. The case must have had some merit as a police office was subsequently opened at 7 Halsall Road.

With the passing of the Parish Highway Board and the coming of the Local Board, the Common never again enjoyed a powerful voice within the local authority. Only four residents ever served as members. In 1877 Samuel Latham, a retired cabinet maker from Shropshire living near the corner of Liverpool and

Clifford Roads, was added to the Local Board without election. A Conservative, the majority looked to him when affairs of the Common were discussed and he invariably gave bland assurances that all was well. In 1881 he was the census enumerator for Birkdale. William Crankshaw, the popular publican of the Crown Hotel, was a Conservative member from 1892. He was a persistent campaigner on behalf of the Common and, as a member of the majority, he enjoyed some success. Walter Marshall, a gardener from 15 Clifford Road, was elected in 1894, when the Common became South Ward. Having achieved success as a Workingman's Candidate he immediately, but unsuccessfully, tried to move a "Fair Contract" resolution. This would have required the Council to pay standard rates to its labourers. Marshall, a radical, later joined the ranks of the *petit bourgeoisie*, becoming a grocer in the shopping centre by Liverpool Road Railway Station.

The concern that Thomas Weld-Blundell had shown in protecting the high-class residential development in Birkdale Park from environmental nuisance was completely absent in his dealing with the Common. He was responsible for several initiatives which could have had an adverse effect on this area. In the 1860s he developed, and subsequently withdrew, a scheme to build a gasworks for Birkdale on the Common. Later, in 1872, the Local Board successfully persuaded him to withdraw a scheme to let land for a brick kiln at Barlow's Crossing, near to the original Birkdale Station.[18] In the same year he negotiated an agreement with the Liverpool Corporation to allow them to tip refuse in the sandhills to the south of the Common. In reply to the predictable outburst he claimed that it would only be dry cinders and scrapings of macadamised roads and, as such, it would not smell much. Critics were not convinced and dubbed it "The Blundell Bouquet".[19] Southport Corporation, fearful of the threat to its bathing beach, joined the Local Board in opposing this scheme and it was withdrawn. This was a rare example of the neighbouring Birkdale and Southport authorities working together.

The old township roads on the Common were private roads, the responsibility of the landowner rather than the Local Board. This proved to be an unhappy arrangement. Both Thomas and Charles Weld-Blundell did little and the Local Board, and later the Council, were unsuccessful in getting them to meet their obligations.

Sandon Road exemplified this neglect. As early as 1871 the Local Board received a memorial from ratepayers on the Common, asking for a better road to the village school. Thomas Weld-Blundell had paved the middle of the road but the footways at the side were completely blocked by blown sand. By 1890 the condition had deteriorated and the whole road was covered by a deep layer of sand. It was down Sandon Road that many of the carts passed, carrying night-soil and manure from the railway sidings to the farms. The night-soil ran through the bottoms of the carts to mix with the sand, thus creating an unwholesome menace to health. In the winter, floods left pools of up to three feet deep in the roadway. The Council attempted to force Charles Weld-Blundell's hand with a notice under the Public Health Act of 1875. After further prevarication, the landowner did make a start on improving the road, but the rate of progress was painfully slow and piles of stones were left in the roadway for months awaiting use, thus adding to the problems. By 1897, gaps between the buildings had been filled but the road's surface remained unmade. Further complaints from the School Committee, the Parish Vestry and warnings from the Council finally appear to have persuaded the landowner to act: or perhaps this was just an act of self-interest for, as will be seen, he was, at this time, trying to promote parts of the Common for building. In 1900 he paid the Council to macadamise Sandon Road. Seven years later it was again pitted with large holes. In 1909 G.L. Stephens, living at number 45, complained that in wet weather pools made it impossible to cross the road directly. Sandon Road was eventually adopted by the Council in 1911. Not without cause did a local commentator suggest that the Council did not seem to have any power over Charles Weld-Blundell.

RESIDENTIAL INFILLING ON THE COMMON

By the census of 1881, the population of the Common had only grown to a little over 1000. Unlike the rest of Birkdale there were still more men than women. The distribution was not skewed here by the presence of female servants, school boarders and annuitants. Sandon Road was typical of the Common, with the census showing that as many as seventeen of the 25 heads of household had been born in the township. Two came from adjoining townships, five from other Lancashire towns, and one from Flintshire. Unlike New Birkdale, the population was still predominantly local in origin, although farming was no longer the dominant occupation. There was only one farm labourer and three farmers listed. The major occupations were general labourers (nine) and gardeners (five). There were no building tradesmen, but perhaps unusually one clerk, T. Crowther, a newcomer from Colne. There were three female heads of household, two of whom were charwomen and one a mat-weaver. Again in 1891 labourers (fifteen) and gardeners (three) constituted the majority of the householders, although there were also two tradesmen – a painter and a plasterer – whilst T. Crowther still lived at number 17. The female heads of household included two charwomen.

The houses in Sandon Road included a row of tiny dwellings which had been built by Birkdale Township in the eighteenth century to house its needy poor. Since the passing of a new Poor Law, this function had transferred to the Guardians in Ormskirk, and what were known as the Union Cottages passed into private ownership. They still survive as two houses. By 1900 another house, number 23, was in such a poor condition that the Council asked its owners – the Ormskirk and Southport Building Society – either to restore or demolish it.

The old labourers' cottages were frequently very small. One typical thatched cottage had external measurements of 24 feet by 12 feet and was 7 feet high.[20] Such new building as took place on the Common was mainly confined to property of the cheapest kind, either for local agricultural workers, or for labourers who were unable to find cheaper accommodation nearer to their work in New Birkdale or Southport. In 1877 a new cottage in Ashton Road was offered at £20 and failed to attract a buyer. It was not until the closing years of the century that a reasonable tramway service was obtained, and then improved by electrification in 1902. The building around 1898 of modest houses, at an annual rental of £19 10s per annum, in Clifford Road, Richmond Road and Liverpool Road, was a result of the enhanced accessibility. In 1905, ten new houses were built around the junction of Sandon Road and Ashton Road. Fourteen new houses were built in Cardigan Road in 1908. By 1911 the Council was asking for extra trams to be put on because of crowding.

One new resident in Cardigan Road, from Manchester, complained about the smoke-laden air. The offending chimneys were those of Birkdale Laundry, a long-standing source of local nuisance, and the newer electricity works, in

Clive Road.

139

Shaftesbury Road. The Council had bought twelve acres near to Todd's Farm for the electricity works. This did not represent Birkdale's conversion to a belief in municipal enterprise, as the Council immediately transferred the site to the British Electric Traction Company, which had to spend £30,000 to build the works. The Company also had to guarantee that the price of electricity in Birkdale would always be lower than that charged in Southport. The Council decided to build a new isolation hospital on part of its Shaftesbury Road site. Opponents of this choice argued, with some merit, that the Council was repeating its previous mistake in locating the isolation hospital in an area which would soon be built-up. They also pointed to the proximity of three dairies. The protests came to naught and the hospital was built. It is interesting to note that, as some of the old smallholdings gave way to bricks and mortar, the Council used the residue of its land in Shaftesbury Road to create 21 small allotments, which it rented out at a shilling a year each.

The building of houses on the 'Little Common', previously open ground at the heart of Old Birkdale, caused periodic protests to both the landowner and to the Council. The Council claimed that, despite the name, it had no record of any common land in Birkdale. This view was confirmed by Weld-Blundell's agent, and supported by W.T. Bulpit, the historian Vicar of Crossens, who stated that the public possessed no rights as to the Common.[21] Sylvia Harrop, however, in *Old Birkdale and Ainsdale*, traces how leases allowing encroachment onto the Common were granted during the early nineteenth century.

There were two shops to serve the isolated Common listed in the 1851 census returns. The growth in population led to an increase in the number and variety of shops. They were mainly situated in and around Liverpool Road. In 1881 there were two shoemakers – Thomas Tomlinson and Joseph Marshall. Thomas Truck ran an ironmonger's shop and John Garstang was the Common's chemist and druggist. Much of the food came from the farms and smallholdings, and the residents still baked their own bread – a bakery only came later. Henry Smith ran a butcher's shop; John Wilding was a provision merchant; while Fred Sykes was a grocer. The Census enumerator also described Fred Sykes as a "bathman". Did he have a large bath, at his premises at 58 Liverpool Road, where the locals went for a good soak on special occasions, or was he a bathchair man?

CHURCHES, CHAPELS, SCHOOLS AND SOCIETIES

The Village School
The Birkdale School in Sandon Road had been rebuilt by Rector Hesketh in 1839. It had not sought grants or affiliation with the National Society, an Anglican body concerned with the provision of elementary schooling for the

children of the lower orders, or with the British Society, which fulfilled a similar function for Nonconformist and religiously independent schools.[22] In 1848 it was reported that:

> . . . the entire control of this village seminary is in the hands of the ratepayers of Birkdale and we believe the school is in a flourishing condition.[23]

By 1851 Cyrus and Cassandra Johnson, the children of Hugh Johnson the former master of the school, were the master and mistress. The Johnsons were a Birkdale family, from farming stock, and were not trained teachers. It is unlikely that they had received any education beyond that available in the village school and the home. Cyrus was the enumerator for the 1851 census, and his returns show almost half of Birkdale's children between the ages of two and fourteen, recorded as 'scholars'. The fact that three were only two, and four aged three years old, was typical of rural schools at this time and suggests that Cassandra performed little beyond a baby-minding role with these young children.

When St. James' C.E. Church was built to serve the new residential area of Birkdale Park in 1857, the middle-class parishioners accepted responsibility for the distant school, which adopted its name. The sponsoring church made an appeal for funds in which the importance of education was stressed ". . . and the great want felt for it among the aborigines of the district."[24] The Boys' and Girls' Schools were located in the one schoolroom and were separated by a curtain hanging from a beam. By 1860 the average attendance was about 60, probably less than a quarter of the children of school-age living on the Common. There was also an evening school conducted in the building, but unfortunately little is known about this early venture in adult education.

The patronage of St. James' Church was reflected in donations and in regular visits paid to the school by the vicar, curate and members of the Committee. Control of their school was passing out of the hands of the villagers of the Common and into those of the new middle-class residents of Birkdale Park. Financial support allowed the appointment, in 1861, of the school's first certificated teacher – John Joel. This 20-year-old bachelor lodged in the School House, then occupied by Henry Ball, a former labourer who became Birkdale's first postman and also was one of the Common's most ardent teetotallers and campaigners for temperance. The mistress was Mary Fisher, an untrained teacher, who had been appointed three years earlier at the age of seventeen. Joel was succeeded in 1867 by Hugh Ashworth, whose wife also taught in the school. He was followed in 1875 by Peter Jones, who enjoyed a long career and was still in office at the end of our period.

From 1861 the school was regularly in receipt of government grant. One condition of receiving annual grant was regular attendance of the scholars.

Attendance at school was not yet compulsory and St. James', like many other schools, experienced great difficulty in securing this. The report of a major government commission, in 1867, described the education of an average boy in this coastal region:

Learns his letters at home, goes to school at nine, and plods away at reading and spelling for a year or two . . . At eleven he is beginning to be of some use in the fields. He is kept away all the time of hay harvest, and of potato picking which follows . . . if near the coast, he is sent out to gather shrimps and cockles. Thus attending school only five or six months in the year, he is unable to make real progress . . . and when he is finally removed from school at thirteen, he has not yet grown familiar enough with the use of the pen to write his name in the marriage register ten years afterwards nor fluent enough in reading to care if he ever opens a book again.[25]

In 1871, the local inspector described St. James' as "almost quite a country school . . . somewhat irregularly attended". Illness, particularly epidemics, could play havoc with attendance. In 1870, the master recorded:

Dorothy Rimmer was sent to school by her parents, although her brother and sister were ill with Scarlet Fever. Separated her from the rest of the scholars.

A week later he noted that Dorothy had died, ". . . after a very short illness." He went on to report: "This is the only case of death which has occurred from a contagious disease this year on Birkdale Common." Three years later an outbreak of diphtheria had more devastating results:

August 11   William Ambrose of the Vth class died yesterday of Diphtheria. Peter Jones of the same class has also been carried off by the same complaint.

August 12   John Marshall of the Vth class absent through Diphtheria.

August 13   Received word that Peet's children are absent through Diphtheria.

August 25   James Leatherbarrow and Peter Peet died during the last week of Diphtheria.

There is a further reference to ". . . attendance being thinned" by the absence of children from the "north end " of Birkdale, ". . . whose parents were afraid of the fever which is prevalent on the Common."

Another contributory factor to poor attendance was the difficulties encountered by parents in finding the money for school fees. Although the fees at St. James' were relatively light – twopence per week – the log books contain many entries about cautions for non-payment and children being sent home.

As the attendance battle was being waged, punctuality became an important

142

issue: the attendance mark, crucial for the earning of government grant, could not be given to latecomers. Many families were handicapped by not having a clock in their home, and in 1879 a Mr. Tuck presented a new bell to St. James' School.

In reviewing the supply of elementary school accommodation in Birkdale, following the Education Act of 1870, it was found that St. James' School had accommodation for 136 children and an average annual attendance of about 100. The Inspector judged that there was a deficiency of 64 places on the Common. With financial support from the wealthy parishioners of Birkdale Park, a new tiered room for the infants was added to the school, and the staff was doubled to four teachers. As the population grew, St. James' School continued to react promptly to demands from the Education Department to increase the number of school places on the Common.

The school's academic record, as measured by performance in the Inspector's annual examinations, was poor. Inspectors repeatedly complained about the teaching – ". . . weakness and unintelligence of the instruction." Although the staff was deemed to be ". . . numerically sufficient", it frequently included too many pupil-teachers and unqualified lady assistants, who were much cheaper to employ than were certificated teachers.

The jobs taken by the leavers reflected not only the limited aspirations of the pupils and the lack of local opportunities, but also the modest level of educational achievement. By 1913, although only two of the eighteen boys leaving went on to agricultural work, the majority went into dead-end jobs – nine became errand boys and two became golf caddies. None went into office work or became shop assistants and only three were apprenticed to a trade.

Churches and Chapels
From its re-building in 1839, the school had also been used as both a Sunday School and a Chapel-of-Ease. In 1849 afternoon services were held at 3pm. It was here that the Rev. Benjamin Swift started his Birkdale ministry in 1850. After the opening of St. James' in Birkdale Park in 1857, the Common became a part of the new parish. The registers show that the residents of the Common used the new church for marriages and baptisms, but, although Swift retained a strong commitment to this poorer part of the parish, it seems they were not members of the congregation. Afternoon services were continued at the school, with the members of St. James' paying for the stipend of a curate there. They also provided a clothing club for the Common. When the new parish of St. Peter's was formed to serve New Birkdale inland of the railway, the Common remained part of the Parish of St. James'.

Initially Swift's successor, Stephenson, did not appear to share his concern for the people of the Common and the afternoon services were allowed to lapse. Later, in response to criticisms, they were resumed. Although the services were sometimes taken by a curate, it seems that it was a layman Charles Foy, of 'Dinorwic House', who conducted the Sunday School and frequently the services, and did much to hold together the congregation on the Common.

As early as 1879, Thomas Weld-Blundell received a deputation from the Rural Deanery concerning the provision of a church for the Common. It appears that he promised to give a site in Clifford Road, but the building fund was slow to grow. By way of explanation, Stephenson pointed to the expenses his Birkdale Park parishioners faced for alterations and repairs at St. James'. He also insisted that money should be raised by donations and not by bazaars or similar events. The delay in raising the money caused complications over the site. Following Thomas Weld-Blundell's death, his son Charles insisted on charging £200 for it, a stark contrast to the generous treatment of those of his own faith. The foundation stone was eventually laid in 1889 by Miss Burton of 'The Warren', in Westcliffe Road. She represented all that was best in Birkdale Park's relationship with the Common, being a popular figure not only because of her generosity to the new church, but also for her regular visiting of parishioners in their homes and for teaching their children in the Sunday School.

The new church, St. John's, was built to a reduced plan, at a cost of £2,620. A feature of the red brick church was its slated bell tower. Despite Stephenson's protestations that the simplicity of the church would appeal to those who, like him, loved the Reformed Church, there appear to have been departures from these principles. There was a decorated altar and plate, which one critic described as "Popish trappings". Uncharacteristically, Stephenson also allowed the installation of stained-glass memorial windows. Annual tea-parties, refused at St. James', were held at St. John's. Although there was a curate in charge, the Bishop refused to consecrate the new church because it had no endowments to support the clergy. He believed that the wealthy parishioners of St. James' could and should provide such a fund, a view shared by the Ecclesiastical Commissioners, who refused to make a grant towards the endowment fund. The issue was resolved by a handsome benefaction from a Mr. Hussey. There were further delays over establishing the boundary between St. John's and St. Peter's parishes. St. John's was finally consecrated in 1904, with the Rev. C. Middleton, a former curate of St. James', as the first vicar. The village school changed its name from St. James' to that of the new parish.

Nonconformity was also strong on the Common. From the early 1850s, Wesleyans met in a cottage at the junction of Shaws Road and Shaftesbury Road. Many of the Marshall family were prominent members of this society, including Thomas Marshall, a cobbler. Henry Ball, the letter carrier, was also a member. By 1884 the society had moved to a cottage off Liverpool Road, close to the site of the present Methodist chapel.[26] Henry Mathwin, the headmaster of

Bickerton House School and one of the Township's leading Methodists, became treasurer of a building appeal for a new chapel. A modest building costing £600 was opened in 1867, at the corner of Liverpool Road and Cardigan Road. This was replaced in 1898 by a new chapel, of deep red brick with facings of buff terracotta, which cost £2,300.

Although there was no Roman Catholic Church on the Common, there was a Catholic reformatory institution for boys – Birkdale Farm School – situated close to the southern boundary of Birkdale with Ainsdale. Although it was well detached from built-up Birkdale, the residents would be aware of the school's presence. The highly disciplined inmates were frequently to be seen parading at local events, whilst its liveried van making daily deliveries of bread from the school's bakery served as a constant reminder. It is interesting to note the high public profile of this penal establishment.

Societies and Feast-Days
There was a strong Burial Club – the Birkdale Club – serving the agricultural workers on the Common. On June 30th 1849, the *Southport Visiter* carried the following report:

> The members of this old established friendly society held their anniversary on Wednesday last. The members paraded the town with that usual accompaniment of festive occasions, – the Churchtown Band – at their head, and finished the day at the clubhouse, the Ash Tree, in Birkdale, by dining off an unlimited supply of the "Roast Beef of Old England" and other necessary accompaniments.

After the opening of St. James' in 1857, the annual feast-day celebrations included a parade through Birkdale Park to the church and then on to the Ash Tree to eat. It seems, however, that the day was so abused by drunkenness that the Rev. Swift withdrew his support and formed a Temperance Club, which held an annual dinner in the schoolroom. In later years this was united with the school "feast-day". The scholars joined the club men in parading through the district; and the rest of the day, after they returned to Birkdale Common, was devoted to games, prize-giving and refreshments. The Vicar and his curate dined with the men and joined in the celebrations. After Swift's resignation the custom lapsed.

Birkdale Feast-Day was subsequently reinstated as the school's annual treat. It was normally held every July, on one of the local farmers' fields, although Victoria Park was later used. The landowner was a subscriber, and on some occasions the treat took the form of an excursion to Ince Blundell Hall. In 1882 eleven wagonettes conveyed 230 children and 50 parents and friends on the two-hour drive. The children were given permission to pick flowers at the Hall, and all the party were served with tea at the Weld-Blundell Arms before commencing the ride home. The *Southport Visiter* described the outing as

". . . creating an amount of excitement in Birkdale Common village, of a kind that is only known in that secluded spot once a year."[27]

Friendly Societies, such as the Birkdale South Tontine Club and the Birkdale Sick and Thrift Club, were set up to insure the inhabitants against hard times. Between 1861 and 1871, the number of gardeners living on the Common increased from five to twelve. By 1881 there were twenty and the local gardeners formed their own Friendly Society. This was obviously a sensitive issue, and a commentator in the *Southport Visiter* explained that:

> It was not meant to be a trade union in any sense of the word, and they had no intention of interfering between employer and employed as to hours, work, wages, or anything else . . . Their Society was purely and simply a benefit society. For a subscription of sixpence a week, sick pay benefit was available and a sum on death.[28]

By 1899, attitudes had changed and a local branch of the Gardeners' Union was inaugurated, with the aim of reducing a 52 hour working week to 50 hours.

Earlier, in 1879, a Birkdale Common Workmen's Social Club had been opened in Cavendish Road. The sponsors included the Vicar of St. James' and the Chairman of the Local Board. The club had over 30 members, paying a weekly subscription of 2d a week. The club's facilities included a reading-room, a games-room, and a smoke-room, and were supervised by a resident manager.

SPORT AND NEW MIDDLE-CLASS RESIDENTIAL DEVELOPMENT

In speculating about the possibility of a new golf club on the Common in 1906, a commentator in the *Southport Visiter* suggested that:

> As each golf course is completed the lots around become automatically the sites of villas, and the garden city can be realised without the pain of propaganda.[29]

Having witnessed the beneficial effect of the presence of the Birkdale Golf Club on residential development in Birkdale Park, it appears that Weld-Blundell thought that creating further courses, inland of the railway, might produce similar results.

In 1906 the formation of a new golf club, the Grosvenor, was announced.[30] A nine-hole course was laid out near to the Common, alongside the Lancashire and Yorkshire Railway line, and the club took its name from nearby Grosvenor Road, on the opposite side of the line in Birkdale Park. The organisers claimed that the fees at Birkdale Golf Club were ". . . in excess of those in other provincial towns, and far in excess of those necessary to maintain a really first class golf course." The new club's fees were set at two guineas a year with a similar joining fee. Within six months there were 140 members and the small course was deemed to be inadequate for their needs. Further extensions to the course were said to be impossible because of adjacent houses and the railway line. A line of houses in the £700 bracket had been built on Dover Road, thus cutting the course off from open land to the south. Negotiations with the landowner quickly produced an alternative. Within six months of its formation the club had secured about 100 acres on the inland side of the railway, between Dover Road and the Birkdale Cemetery. The new course would thus form a link with Ainsdale, where Weld-Blundell had striven so hard to stimulate a new residential town, and was called Southport and Ainsdale Golf Club. The land was described as having natural hazards and splendid land formations, and a course of over 6,000 yards was laid out. In the absence of Weld-Blundell, the course was opened by his agent, C.J. Skitt, in 1907. The captain of the Club thanked the landowner for letting them have the links on such good terms. Weld-Blundell's generosity did not, however, extend to a long lease. Flexibility, for the landlord, was everything in emerging residential districts. The new clubhouse consisted of a pair of semi-detached villas, at 348 and 350 Liverpool Road, some 100 yards from the tramway terminus at the Crown Hotel. This clubhouse was vacated and the adjoining land lost in the 1920s, when Waterloo Road was built.

The clubhouse was part of a line of imposing villas built about this time. The area south of the Crown Hotel was known as Birkdale South End. The country

Crown Hotel, Liverpool Road.

pub, which had served the agricultural community, had been rebuilt in 1898, and had been joined to the south by a number of substantial semi-detached houses. Farnborough Road was made and sewered in 1905. Here were the beginnings of a new residential development, which Weld-Blundell wished to become a continuous line of property between Birkdale and Ainsdale. As well as the presence of the golf club, the extended and improved tramway was a critical factor in this scheme. The *Southport Visiter* speculated that, when Ainsdale was amalgamated with Birkdale in 1905, the tramway would surely be extended down Liverpool Road to Ainsdale. In an attempt to improve the Liverpool Road link between Birkdale and Ainsdale, Weld-Blundell offered to give the Council a nine-foot-wide strip of land to form a pavement south of the Crown Hotel. This uncharacteristically generous offer, and his presence when a Council deputation inspected the site, were an indication of his anxiety to secure this development. It was in stark contrast to the cavalier fashion in which he had long treated the Council and the people of the Common, in his neglect of the roads and pavements.

Birkdale's cemetery also figured in the development occurring at the southern end of the township. Victorian cemeteries were popular social amenities. Elegantly laid out, their paths were used by promenaders as well as those intent on paying their respects to the departed. Birkdale had been a part of the parish of North Meols and it was in the graveyard of the distant parish church of St. Cuthbert's that its dead were formerly buried. A party of mourners would share carrying the coffin for its five-mile journey from the Common. In his *Notes on Southport and District* Bulpit tells of "The Breeing Stone", which marked the boundary with Southport, where mourners rested and the coffin was sprinkled with rainwater from a hollow in the stone.

Birkdale's new church, St. James', did not have a churchyard and the Rector of North Meols continued to allow burials of Birkdale residents in Churchtown. In 1865 Southport opened a new cemetery, quite close to its boundary with Birkdale. This provided Birkdale residents with a more convenient alternative to Churchtown, although the burial charge was a guinea higher than for residents of Southport. There the matter rested until 1881, when, following an approach from the Birkdale Local Board, Charles Weld-Blundell offered a 10-acre plot for a cemetery opposite to the Birkdale Farm School, near to the boundary with Ainsdale. The asking price was £2,000, and the Board dithered and dallied. Critics of the scheme argued that the site was in a wilderness, remote from Birkdale, with poor road links. Following a close vote the Board accepted the offer in 1885. A Liberal councillor later made an unsubstantiated accusation that a Conservative member had received a "backhander" from Weld-Blundell for his support. Weld-Blundell stood to gain far more than the purchase price; a cemetery was a social amenity which could help to transform the surrounding area.

What happened next was another of Birkdale's municipal mysteries. Having borrowed the £2,000 for the site, on which interest charges had to be paid, nothing further was done about the cemetery until the turn of the century. Then in another expression of its new vitality, the Council obtained a loan of £4,000, with which the cemetery was handsomely laid out and finally brought into use in 1903, almost 20 years after the land had been bought.

Birkdale South End had other qualities which were less attractive in a residential area. The ribbon development of Liverpool Road was taking place on farm land, and farming was still going on in adjoining fields. In 1889 E.M. Maude, a new resident, wrote a letter to the *Southport Visiter* complaining that:

> A farmer who has some fields at the back of the Crown Hotel has caused to be laid over them several railway loads of night soil as a surface dressing amounting to sixty tons. The smell is shocking and making people feel very ill. I am told that all the farmers here lay this filth over their land. If so I shall move at once.[31]

Such letters were common: another accused John Marshall of Sutton's Farm, also near the Crown Hotel, of spreading night-soil within 70 yards of property. The Medical Officer complained annually about the particularly offensive night-soil – Oldham Shoddy – used on this farm. The railway company was unsuccessfully asked not to transport it.[32] Adding to the stench was the presence of the 'piggeries' on the inland side of Liverpool Road. Nevertheless, this large pig farm, complete with cooking and hanging sheds, was given a clean bill of health by the Medical Officer.

Local children were another source of annoyance to new residents. They had traditionally played on the road, and the coming of the tramway had made this a dangerous practice. In 1905 the Water Board offered to let the Council have a small half-acre plot of land in Liverpool Road South, north of the Crown Hotel, for use as a recreation ground. This was a former pipeyard which was surplus to the Water Board's requirements. The Council accepted the offer and paid an annual rent of £5. Six seats and some swings were installed. South End Recreation Ground succeeded in getting children off the road, but was soon itself the subject of a memorial to the Council complaining about noise and rowdy behaviour, particularly by youths. As a result, the Council appointed a keeper to superintend the small ground for two hours each evening and its use was confined to children of school age. The site later reverted to the Water Board and is still used by North West Water.

The links vacated by the Grosvenor Golf Club did not remain unused for long. W.A. Findlay, a Scottish doctor in Southport, rented the course in his own name. He formed the Blundell Golf Club with the object of providing golf without ". . . burdening the members with the heavy expenses usually associated with the game." With an annual fee of only one guinea, the Club quickly recruited over 100 members. Many took advantage of the railway to travel from Liverpool. Several adjoining fields were added to the course and the holes lengthened. Despite these improvements the Blundell Club transferred to new links in Ainsdale in 1911. Apparently this move was a further attempt by Weld-Blundell to use golf to fertilise residential development and to promote Ainsdale.

Residents of Dunkirk Road feared that houses would be built on the site of the old Blundell links alongside the railway and petitioned the Council to retain it as an open space. In the event it quickly became the home of yet another Birkdale golf club – Hillside. This new club leased the land from Peter Lloyd of Hillside Farm and apparently decided to use this name in its title. The enclosing of what was widely believed to have been common land, and its use for golf, was unsuccessfully challenged by some residents. In the 1920s the Hillside Golf Club migrated across the railway to its present course, where the links were to achieve championship status.

Meanwhile, building around the nine-hole course continued, and the residents pressed the railway company to place a station near to the site of the original Birkdale Station. It was claimed that there were now 660 houses in the vicinity. The Birkdale, Southport and Ainsdale and Hillside golf clubs all stood to benefit from the opening of such a conveniently situated station and joined the clamour. It was suggested that the name of "Birkdale Links" might be appropriate. Charles Weld-Blundell, the Birkdale Park Land Company, and the Council added their support but the railway company remained unmoved, refusing to countenance the expense of building a second station and a crossing in Birkdale.

Whilst golf, a middle-class sport which helped to further Weld-Blundell's residential ambitions, flourished in Birkdale, football, a working-class sport, was positively discouraged by the landowner. Minor football teams, frequently attached to church or chapel and playing in the local leagues, were a feature of Birkdale. During the 1890s a different kind of football club emerged on the Common. It was the well-supported Birkdale South End. William Crankshaw, the publican of the Crown Hotel, was the secretary and organiser. The club played successfully in the Liverpool Combination, and in 1893 won the Southport Junior Cup in front of a crowd of 750. The club claimed to be strictly amateur, with no professional players, but it did take gate income. Despite its success, or perhaps because of it, the club ran into difficulties over a ground. Although popular with the community, it was not favoured by Charles Weld-Blundell. He was prepared to lease land for golf courses but was absolutely opposed to granting land for use as a football ground. Indeed, his later book reveals that he had a strong antipathy towards the game: ". . . where professionals play for money and idlers in their thousands look on."[33] Unlike golf, football and particularly football supporters did not fit the image of the changes he was promoting around the Common. He refused a request from

Birkdale South End for land for a ground, and then instructed the farmer on whose land South End played in Richmond Road, to get rid of them as soon as possible. Richmond Road was on the fringe of his expanding middle-class development in New Birkdale. Further building was taking place in Clifford Road West (later St. John's Road). Any spectators walking from the populous Chatham and Kew Road area would have to pass through his new Dinorwic Estate. Crankshaw appealed to his colleagues on the Council for the use of the Recreation Ground (Victoria Park). This the Council refused, on the grounds that the covenant would not allow the creation of an enclosed ground, to which an entrance fee would be charged. The hidden agenda was the fact that football supporters trooping across Birkdale Park would not have been welcome. South End had enjoyed a decade of playing success, regularly attracting hundreds of spectators, many of whom followed the team to away games. It seems that this support did not extend to Birkdale's landowner and legislators, and the club faded.

By 1911 Birkdale Common had lost its dependence upon agriculture, although many of the old families still lived in the area. The heart of the Common was becoming a lower working-class dormitory, with the beginnings of a new middle-class suburb to the south around the golf courses, and an infilling of upper working-class dwellings to the north, between the Common and the middle-class property of east Birkdale.

CHAPTER EIGHT

BIRKDALE'S BATTLES OF THE BEACH

An enterprising landlord who invests capital to reclaim waste land and wins land from the sea, finds he must run the gauntlet of Royal Privilege and Crown Rights if land is to be reclaimed along the seashore; or else the jealous opposition of a parish council, usually prodded by an active and ingenious Radical lawyer, leads to a call to down trodden commoners to rise in their thousands and preserve their cherished rights.

Charles Weld-Blundell
letter to *The Morning Post*, October 1905

Questions of ownership and of rights on the foreshore were the subject of continuing controversy during this period. Thomas Weld-Blundell's rights to wreck were admitted by the Board of Trade under the Merchant Shipping Act of 1854. Nevertheless, he contested the claim that the rights of the Port of Liverpool extended across his land as far as Hesketh Bank.[1] Although fishing figured prominently in the "Battles of the Beach", it was only a token issue through which principles could be established.

For the Weld-Blundells, particularly Charles, the real stakes were much higher. For the purposes of stake-net fishing, the Birkdale foreshore had historically been split into four large units, called "stalls". Details of local practice and the leasing of these stalls are given by Sylvia Harrop in *Old Birkdale and Ainsdale*. During the first half of the nineteenth century strict supervision of the foreshore had lapsed, and Southport fishermen were trespassing and setting nets on Birkdale beach. The principal catch was mackerel, a most unpredictable fish. Sometimes not one was caught, whilst at other times they were so plentiful they had to be carted away for manure. The best catches were associated with off-shore breezes, when the mackerel came in-shore in search of small herrings and sand-eels.

Early in Thomas Weld-Blundell's stewardship of his estates, he demonstrated his determination to re-assert his manorial rights on the

152

foreshore. From 1849, he encouraged his tenants to try to prevent the Southport fishermen from trespassing. One tenant stated that:

> They (Southport fishermen) are upon my stall for which I pay £2 10s a year – I have nets down now and these men set their nets before mine so that no fish can get into my nets.

Another alleged that:

> Repeated notices have been given to them to withdraw; but they have refused to do so and in some cases have taken entire possession of stalls belonging to tenants of Mr. Weld-Blundell . . . contending the right to fish there is common to all.[2]

Such a view was anathema to the Lord of the Manor. In order to confirm his legal rights he instructed his solicitor to examine the Court Book of the Manor of Birkdale from beginning to end.[3] Meanwhile, his tenants (possibly incited by him) used force to repel the Southport men, and a case of assault against them came before the Southport Petty Sessions on the 12th of July 1858. Miles Livesey, a Weld-Blundell tenant, was fined 2 shillings with costs, but Weld-Blundell's rights had been re-established.

In 1881, when the lagoons in front of Westcliffe Road were giving off a stench, the Birkdale Local Board recognised Weld-Blundell's ownership of the beach, when it made an unsuccessful appeal to him to fill them in. About the same time he laid a light railway across the beach to transport sand. The ultimate practical test of his ownership was, however, his transfer of land for the building of the Southport and Cheshire Line Extension Railway, and his gift to the Birkdale Local Board of the re-claimed land for Rotten Row, the Esplanade and Victoria Park. Content that his rights were recognised, Weld-Blundell permitted the Birkdale Local Board to exercise a degree of supervision of activities on the foreshore. It was allowed to regulate bathing, and in 1884 the Board turned down a request for a photographic booth on the foreshore.

There also appears to have been a period of relative peace for the fishermen up to the accession of Charles Weld-Blundell in 1887, after which there was an upsurge in activity. In 1890 the right of Marshside fishermen to cross Birkdale beach, as they made their way to fish for shrimps, was challenged. Weld-Blundell's ranger took their names with a view to summonses for trespass. The fishermen, who held a protest meeting at Southport's Temperance Hall, claimed that they had fished uninterrupted off Birkdale beach for 60 years by hand (putting) and by boats (shanking), and that only the use of horse-drawn carts crossing the beach was new.

The question of rights on the foreshore had earlier become a lively issue in adjoining Southport. In 1883 a legal difficulty arose, when Southport Corporation was challenging the construction of the training walls for the Ribble Channel, in the Ribble Navigation Bill. There appeared to be uncertainty about the relative rights of the Lords of the Manor and the Duchy of Lancaster. The Lords of the Manor – Charles Hesketh and Charles Scarisbrick – swiftly acted to purchase such rights as the Duchy held. Subsequently, all rights held by the Lords of the Manor to the foreshore were sold by them to the Southport Corporation, on the condition that the land in front of the town should not be built on other than for recreational purposes. Presumably Scarisbrick and Hesketh inserted this requirement in the interests of their extensive existing estates in Southport.

The ambiguity about ownership and rights was just as relevant in Birkdale. The confusion was apparent in an attempt by the Birkdale Local Board Surveyor to describe the position:

> The sea or foreshore in or opposite Birkdale, within or without the District of the Birkdale Local Board, as the case may be, the property of the said Charles Weld-Blundell or the Queen's most excellent Majesty in the rights of the Duchy of Lancaster, or both or one of them.[4]

The final meeting of the Birkdale Local Board, before it was superseded by the Urban District Council in 1894, was to produce a bombshell. The Chairman announced the purchase from the Duchy of Lancaster of the rights the Duchy held for Birkdale foreshore. Weld-Blundell had not been consulted, and knew nothing of this transaction until he later read of it in the Board's Minutes. As the purchaser was the local authority, the price was a nominal sum of £50, compared with the £15,000 paid by the Lords of the Manor for the Duchy rights at Southport. The Duchy Office declared that it had made the sale ". . . for the purpose of better safeguarding the rights of the public and securing their more advantageous enjoyment."[5]

There were now active rival claimants for the ownership of Birkdale foreshore – the landowner and the Council. Following the death, in 1896, of eight-year-old James Costa whilst bathing at low-water, the Coroner recommended the erection of warning notices on the beach. Boards were put up by the Council, but Weld-Blundell's agent had them pulled out and then thrown down on the sand to be washed away by the tide. One councillor suggested that a prosecution should be issued, but Weld-Blundell's challenge to the Council's authority went unanswered. Weld-Blundell further exercised his authority by ordering the Council to stop depositing cinders on the beach.

Birkdale Council was reluctant to enter into litigation against Charles Weld-Blundell. The landowner had prepared himself for battle and was armed with an extensive and detailed opinion from counsel. The records of Weld-Blundell's solicitor show that this was based on the earlier exhaustive search through the Court Book. His Counsel, Mr. Stuart Moore, confidently expressed the view that the relevant grants of the Barony of Penwortham had passed to Weld-Blundell. In 1900 critics charged the Birkdale Council with looking calmly on

154

whilst Weld-Blundell erected notice boards forbidding the taking of sand from the foreshore. There was a further challenge, in 1901, when he laid another light railway across the beach, to transport materials to Ainsdale. On this occasion, several councillors unsuccessfully urged the Council to take action. In contrast, Weld-Blundell was, as ever, quick to have recourse to the law. In 1901 a case was brought against a Southport man who took some wreckage from the beach. Peace between the landowner and the local authority was restored when Weld-Blundell became Chairman of the Birkdale Council, but it was on his terms. In 1903 he gave the Council permission to plant brushwood on the foreshore in an experiment to prevent sand drifting onto the Esplanade. He insisted, however, that the Council should formally acknowledge that it was doing so with his consent.[6] In the following year, he took the Birkdale Council to the Liverpool Chancery Court over a pipeline on the foreshore. It transpired that it had been placed there twelve years earlier with the simple purpose of carrying away surface water. On this occasion Weld-Blundell withdrew the case, but he had put down a marker to indicate his growing opposition to a sea outfall for a Birkdale sewerage scheme.

Around the turn of the century trespassing on fishing stalls was again rife. In 1905 the Estate Office decided to re-survey the shore and employed Ralph Brook, an old fisherman, to stake out new lots. The previous survey had been done thirteen years earlier. The eight new lots were smaller than the four old stalls, and, in a growing awareness of fish stock conservation, the Board of Trade insisted on a gap of 150 yards between each. On each 400 yard wide lot, a net five feet high and up to 600 yards long was set at an angle. The staked net had a cord top and bottom and it was marked with buoys. The north end of the net was called the "bun", whilst the end in the shallow water was known as the "baulk". The Lancashire Sea Fisheries Committee regulated the mesh size. The nominal rent for the lot was half-a-crown a year and for this the Estate Office undertook to defend fishermen from predatory incursions. Weld-Blundell's rangers were quick to cut down unlicensed nets. Five Birkdale fishermen, along with three from Southport, took licences. The Birkdale men were: Thomas and Richard Moore of Shaftesbury Road, William Carr of Bedford Road, Edward Carr of Liverpool Road South, and Thomas Rimmer of Sandon Road. Licences were also issued to two cockle gatherers – James Ainsbury and Thomas McCain of Stamford Road.[7]

In the following year, in what appeared to be an uncharacteristic display of bravado, the Council decided to assert what it believed to be its rights, purchased from the Duchy. Advertisements were placed in the Southport papers announcing that it was to issue licences for stake-net fishing. These licences had the authority of the Birkdale Council seal stamped on them. Interestingly, the first five licenses issued were all to residents of Southport.

Weld-Blundell issued a counter-notice, setting forth his contention that he

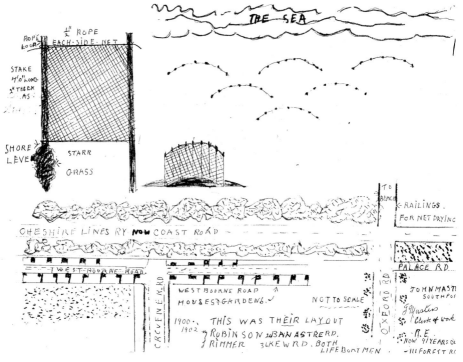

Birkdale Beach: plan of fishing lots, c. 1901.

was the owner of the fisheries and warning fishermen accordingly. As was his wont he issued a writ against the Council. Meanwhile, he had the foreshore patrolled by uniformed rangers. It was claimed that they intimidated people walking on the shore, stopping them to inform them that they were trespassing. Notwithstanding, the Council continued to issue fishing licences.

Weld-Blundell commenced an action in the High Court for a declaration of his rights on the foreshore. This appeared to strike terror into the hearts of Birkdale Councillors. They were afraid of the possible cost of contesting Weld-Blundell's claim, and of the impact of such a cost on the rates. Negotiations were commenced between the two parties. Weld-Blundell's personal interest in this affair is the probable explanation for the unusual amount of time he spent in Birkdale during this period. The Council went through one of its most bizarre periods, casting a shroud of secrecy over the whole matter during two years of wrangling. An agreement was finally reached on the fourth of February, 1908, but the terms were not divulged for fear of the electoral consequences. Such was the secrecy surrounding these negotiations that not all the councillors were shown the details. Rumour was rife, especially concerning the rights of individual access to the beach. The agreement was said to forbid people from "lingering" on the foreshore. The secrecy finally came to an end in June 1909, when Weld-Blundell, much to the annoyance of the Council, published the full terms in his own magazine *The Birkdale Pioneer*. The Council appeared to have meekly surrendered. The Birkdale Council's rights to the foreshore had been transferred to Weld-Blundell. In addition, on his insistence, the Council had purchased the remaining Duchy rights, which included those to mining, minerals, wrecks, and interestingly fishing, for £500, and for the same sum it then sold them to him. What did Birkdale get in return? Weld-Blundell gave the Council the six acres of duneland to make Bedford Park. His conditions included the requirement for them to enclose the land, pay for road-making, level the site and lay it out in an attractive manner. Thus his "gift" would enhance the value of his adjoining land at no cost to himself. Furthermore, he was no longer responsible for clearing the sand which persistently blew from these hills into the adjoining roads and properties. Charles was in his mid-sixties and was anxious to involve his son – Richard, who was still a student at Oxford – in the management of the estate. The agreement had to await ratification until Richard came of age. It was to be over six months after this event before the documents were finally exchanged in April 1909.

An immediate sign that peace had arrived was the landowner giving the Council permission to erect notices warning of the dangers of bathing. Individual freedom to use the beach had not been removed. The terms allowed rowing, riding, walking and bathing. Shooting and fishing were regulated.

The public issue for the foreshore dispute was fishing, but the underlying motive was Weld-Blundell's awareness of the potential for future building on re-claimed land. He had also insisted on the Council obtaining the mineral rights for him. Had he anticipated an Irish Sea oil field? The agreement even left open the possibility of him building a port or harbour. An engineer had costed a scheme for a protected harbour at Ainsdale at £200,000.[8] He was clearly keeping all his options open. An indication of the fertility of his mind was an attempt, in 1904, to develop oyster beds off Ainsdale. He employed a French expert, who came to live in the district. Pools, with piped water, were created in the slacks of the sand dunes for the cultivation of young oysters. The oysters were imported from Arcachon, on Les Landes in the Bay of Biscay. Over two million were laid on the beach.[9] Unfortunately they rapidly vanished as the strong current scoured them away. A more enduring memorial to his initiative were the thousands of pine trees he planted at Freshfield. These transformed the landscape and created what was to become an important red squirrel reserve. There could be no more appropriate outcome for a landowner whose crest included a squirrel cracking a nut. His purpose in planting trees was not merely cosmetic. In his book *What's Wrong with England*, he described:

> The provision of wide belts not less than seventy to eighty yards in width, defending the intending farms or holdings from the prevailing winds, and if by the sea, sheltering growing plants from the destructive effect of saline winds.[10]

Weld-Blundell's vision for his Estate was not one of nature reserves, open spaces, or even farms. He envisaged a coastal residential town extending from Southport to Formby. Detailed plans show a vast urban development, immodestly called "Charlesville", linking Ainsdale to Formby. The principal feature of his grand design was a Marine Drive, six miles long and 60 feet wide, lined with trees, with Ainsdale at its centre. In 1901 he made a start on this boulevard, from Oxford Road. He chose to use the narrow strip of ground between the Cheshire Lines Railway, now the Coastal Road, and the rear garden walls of the villas in Westbourne Road. Virtually all these walls contained a gate, a right included in many of the leases. These gave quick access to the Birkdale Palace Station and to the beach. Weld-Blundell fenced the area, placed gates at the end, erected a watchman's hut and had the area guarded by rangers in uniform. The residents were incensed and unsuccessfully approached the Council.

The action was taking place on the seaward side of the Birkdale Park Land Company's 250 acres. Its property had precisely defined inland boundaries, but the Company now initiated a legal action contesting this western boundary. Weld-Blundell's position was that when the land was sold to the Land Company the rear walls of the houses on Westbourne Road were the high water mark, and thus the limit of its property. He was supported by expert witnesses: Richard Roberts, a labourer born in Birkdale, gave evidence on the extent of the tides 60 years earlier; whilst Thomas Mellor Reid, a civil engineer who had made a survey for Thomas Weld-Blundell in 1871, confirmed that, at that time, the back walls were the limit of the tide wash. The Land Company's case failed, thus confirming that the enclosed land and that on which the railway was built was reclaimed land, belonging to the Lord of the Manor.

The plans for the Marine Drive show an attractively landscaped sea-front boulevard. This was not designed to cater for excursionists from Southport: it was intended to open up building land for further residential development. The confidential letter that Southport's Town Clerk wrote to Weld-Blundell in 1903 seeking his support for amalgamation, demonstrates that he understood this. On behalf of the Southport Council, he offered to finance the building of the Marine Drive to Ainsdale, pointing out that it would open up vast areas of Weld-Blundell's sand dunes for building. This very tempting "sweetener" disappeared with the collapse of Southport's case at the amalgamation inquiry.

Despite his attempts to develop middle-class residential areas east of the Lancashire and Yorkshire Railway Company line and in Ainsdale, Weld-Blundell realised that the premium location was Birkdale Park, adjoining the Southport boundary. The further the distance of property from the amenities of Southport, the lower its value. The only undeveloped land he had west of the railway was to the south, beyond the Land Company's 250 acres. It was for this reason that he was attracted by the potential of the foreshore for development.

The commercial motive which underlay Charles Weld-Blundell's intransigent attitude towards his rights on the foreshore was finally revealed when he submitted plans to the Birkdale Council in August 1911 for a grand and very controversial building scheme. The chosen site was adjoining Southport – the area flanking the Esplanade and the Cheshire Lines Railway had been used, for the previous 40 years, as a summer camp for poor boys from the Manchester district; whilst on the seaward side of the Esplanade accretion had let to the formation of a belt of sand dunes. Despite the planting of starr grass, blown sand from these dunes perpetually engulfed the Esplanade. He proposed to enclose this area with a new Marine Drive, which would have been an extension of Southport's Marine Drive. He intended to build an estate

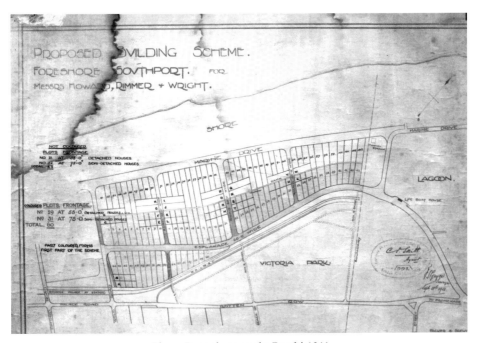

Plan – Bungalows on the Beach! 1911.

of 100 detached and semi-detached dormer bungalows, 82 of which were to be on the seaward side of the Esplanade. This threat to the Frontagers' sea view brought an apoplectic reaction. It was argued that the new houses, with less than £100 a year letting value, would seriously affect the value of the great villas in Westcliffe Road and neighbourhood. The interests of these residents, who were owners of large properties and thus major ratepayers, were facing yet another attack.

A half-page advertisement in the *Southport Visiter*, on 9th September 1911, described the development as a garden village within a garden town. It claimed that the adjacent site was washed by the rolling tide every day, whilst, from their front windows and verandahs, residents would have a view of a vast expanse of sunlit sea and sky. The proximity to Birkdale Golf Club was pointed out. The bungalows were to be placed in half-acre plots. It was argued that bungalows would not obstruct the view from Westcliffe Road. The plots had been let to three local builders and Ball and Percival were to act as agent. The intention was to double the width of the Esplanade, give it a broad tiled pavement and boulevard it with trees. It was claimed that the total scheme would cost £500,000. This figure has all the appearance of developer's hyperbole. The advertisement also proclaimed that, if the Birkdale Council approved, work would be in hand before the winter.

There were some supporters of the development on the Council. E.A. Hodge, a Liberal, thought that the generous landowner had come up with an excellent scheme, which would make Birkdale beautiful and carry it nearer to the sea. Another Councillor, A.W. Ross, was the solicitor to the syndicate working with Weld-Blundell. Predictably, however, the Council received a number of letters of protest. Weld-Blundell was anxious to get approval and proceed before the imminent amalgamation of Birkdale with Southport, but the Council appeared nervous about sanctioning such a major initiative at this time. After consulting the Southport Town Clerk, Birkdale's Health and Plans Committee turned the plans down on technical grounds – The Southport and Cheshire Lines Extension Railway Act of 1882 included restrictive covenants forbidding the erection of buildings on the Esplanade. Practical objections about sanitation were also raised and the Council agreed to defer the scheme to allow the new authority for greater Southport to consider it, after amalgamation.

The developers did not wait. With less than a month to go to amalgamation, Weld-Blundell's agent wrote to the Birkdale Council giving notice that it was the Estate's intention to lay a water supply line across the Esplanade to allow the builders to carry out their operations. At the same time Cook and Talbot, the solicitors for the builders – William Rimmer, John Howard, and Nicholas Wright – wrote to the Council announcing that they intended to proceed with the erection of three dwelling houses notwithstanding the objections of the Plans Committee, which in their view were unwarranted and invalid. Their

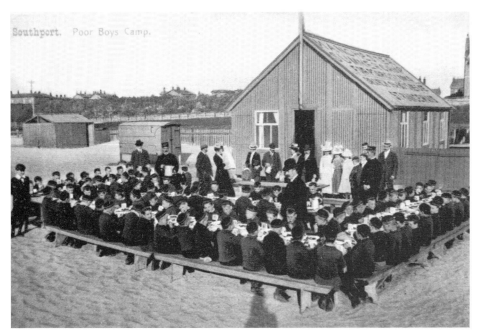

Poor Boys' Camp.

clients were, they asserted, prepared to reply to any proceedings taken by the Council.

Guided by Jarratt, their capable Town Clerk, the Southport Council did not wait for amalgamation. Action was immediate and decisive. The Town Planning Act of 1909 was used to kill the initiative, and Southport produced an alternative scheme for Birkdale's sea front. The camp for poor boys remained; sand hills continued to form in front of the Esplanade, and spill over onto it. The notion of building in this area lay dormant until some eighty years later, when a similar proposal to build houses on this section of the seafront appeared in a Sefton Council development plan. This scheme faced a barrage of environmental protest and was quietly withdrawn. The foreshore had been purchased from the Estate by the local authority for £10,000 in 1928. Few of the protestors realised that the battle had been fought before and had been a very close-run affair. With landowner and local authority both having failed in their attempts to build in this area, the Birkdale Civic Society have stepped in and developed an attractive nature reserve. Nevertheless, the area remains a tempting target for housing development and it is doubtful whether the final chapter in this saga has yet been written.

CHAPTER NINE

NEW BIRKDALE: SOME CONCLUSIONS AND COMPARISONS

Although it experienced over half a century of independent existence, New Birkdale was always a suburb of Southport. Prior to the nineteenth century, the Parish of North Meols on the south-west Lancashire coast had been a rural backwater, relatively isolated from the rest of the county. It consisted of two townships – North Meols and Birkdale. Churchtown, in the north, was the principal village and the site of the ancient parish church. The rest of the parish, including Birkdale, was sparsely populated. Then a major upheaval took place in the first half of the nineteenth century. The rural life of the Township of North Meols was disrupted by the rapid growth within it of the seaside resort of Southport. The dispute over succession to the Blundell Estate meant that Birkdale did not share in this dramatic suburban development. A new Township of Southport was created by an Improvement Act of 1846, whilst to the north, the original village of Churchtown and its rural surrounds remained in the much reduced Township of North Meols. In addition to facilitating holiday traffic, new rail communications, built about mid-century, reinforced the emergence of Southport as a residential town for the wealthy.

Southport's urban development came to an artificially abrupt end at its southern boundary with Birkdale. It was only after the vexed family question of the ownership of Birkdale was resolved, that development also took place there. Thomas Weld-Blundell, the new landowner, was anxious to emulate the success that the Scarisbrick and Hesketh families had enjoyed with their estates in Southport. From the outset, his intention was to create a high-class residential suburb – Birkdale Park. He was able to offer would-be tenants most of the basic requirements for the success of such a scheme: social seclusion, rail transport, a healthy smoke-free location and a plan to landscape the area. His original design, however, showed development centering on a new Birkdale Park Railway Station in Weld Road. Market forces dictated that Birkdale Park did not develop in this way, independently of Southport, but rather as an

Lord Street Boulevard.

integral part of Southport's zonal pattern of development. It grew outward from the town-centre as a suburb of Southport. Southport provided Birkdale Park residents with social facilities, churches, a wide range of shops, and above all Lord Street, the most fashionable boulevard in Lancashire. Without the availability of these Southport amenities it is highly unlikely that New Birkdale would have happened at all.

Other attempts to promote high-class residential estates, nearer to Liverpool, illustrate the critical importance of such amenities. Shortly after the opening of the Liverpool to Southport railway, an attempt was made to create an exclusive high-class residential district on the seaward side of Formby Station. The site enjoyed a convenient rail link to Liverpool, social seclusion, and a smoke-free aspect. Churches were considered a vital amenity for middle-class areas and St. Luke's Church was opened in 1855. The Consecration programme optimistically forecast that: "A great increase in population is expected to take place."[1] Unlike Birkdale Park, however, Formby could not offer prospective tenants the range of amenities available in Southport. The high hopes of the promoters were not realised, and for many years St. Luke's remained an isolated folly amongst the sand dunes.

There were further abortive attempts to accelerate residential development in Formby. In 1875 a group of Southport businessmen launched a company with £50,000 of capital, and put forward an ambitious plan for a new town, "Formby-on-Sea",[2] whilst further north Charles Weld-Blundell later proposed similar schemes for "Freshfield-on-Sea" and "Ainsdale-on-Sea". All these areas had to wait until the second half of the twentieth century before they developed as extensive commuter dormitories.

Rather more successful were the endeavours of the Blundell family of Little Crosby, further south at Blundellsands. The Blundells owned land at Crosby, at the northern extremity of the Liverpool conurbation. William Blundell was the Chairman of the Liverpool, Crosby and Southport Railway. He offered to give the Railway Company the land it required, free of cost, for the line's passage through his property. He did, however, successfully impose a condition. He wanted the line to be brought through the barren coastal strip, rather than further inland through the old agricultural villages of Great and Little Crosby. It was part of the vast rabbit warren, on the seaward side of the railway, that William's son Nicholas set about developing as a high-class residential suburb. Blundellsands, as it quickly became known, enjoyed many of the features essential to the success of a high-class residential suburb. Its river-side site was blessed with magnificent views across the estuary with the mountains of North Wales in the background, whilst the on-shore south-westerlies ensured an unpolluted atmosphere. Social seclusion was well preserved. As at Birkdale, the railway line provided an inland barrier and there was no road linking Blundellsands to Waterloo to the north. Access to Blundellsands was limited to a single gated road, which ran inland over the railway. As in Birkdale, the ownership of the land by a single landowner enabled Nicholas Blundell to preserve the exclusive nature of this high-class residential area, by imposing covenants on the leases. The site did have some limitations: it was very exposed to the wind and houses were later lost to the fast-flowing and changing channel of the Mersey Estuary.

Although the first lease was signed in 1854, development was much slower than in Birkdale and by 1861 there were only five properties in Blundellsands.[3] Nicholas employed the same Liverpool architects who had made the plan for the second phase of Birkdale Park and their similar design for Blundellsands featured a wide, gently curving road – The Serpentine. As in Birkdale, the roads were asphalted to give a much quieter surface than the cobbles in normal use. In 1873, when the sale of plots was sluggish, Nicholas sold a block of land to a Land Company and thus raised instant capital – the same device as used by Weld-Blundell in Birkdale. Blundellsands benefited from being an outer suburb of Liverpool, but was handicapped by not having easy access to social facilities and amenities, such as those enjoyed by Birkdale residents in Southport.

During the second half of the nineteenth century, Birkdale Park was the most successful of the high-class residential areas on the south-west Lancashire coast. As Blundellsands, Formby, Freshfield and Ainsdale were all nearer to Liverpool, and all had similar characteristics to offer to residents, the explanation would appear to lie in Birkdale Park's role as a suburb of Southport. Indeed, an article in the *Liverpool Porcupine* described Southport in the 1880s as ". . . the richest town in the world in proportion to its population", whilst the *Bootle Times* referred to the town as: "A monument representing the energy and industry of Lancashire people."[4] It was the amenities of this prosperous seaside residential town that the residents of Birkdale Park were able to share. That Southport and Birkdale shared a common cultural and social life was further evidenced by the number of clubs and societies which had the prefix "Southport and Birkdale" in their title. These covered such diverse activities as Cricket, Philharmonic, Amateur Operatic, Horticultural, Gardening, Canine, Provident, District Nursing, Anti-Vivisection, Total Abstinence, and Social and Moral Questions. In the fourteen years preceding 1890 there was an independent Birkdale Musical Society, but in that year it was merged into a Southport and Birkdale Musical Society.

Birkdale was historically an independent township in the Parish of North Meols. Initially it was administered through the Parish Vestry. Many early residents of Birkdale Park had not wanted to be administratively linked to the inland agricultural area of Birkdale fearing political domination by the farmers, who had a very different agenda. In 1863 the Local Government Board decided on an independent Local Board for the whole of Birkdale, rather than amalgamation of Birkdale Park with Southport. The Birkdale Local Board quickly became the instrument of Birkdale Park's wealthy residents, on whose rates it depended. The principal policy aim of this low-key authority was to keep the rates lower than those levied across the boundary in Southport. Geographically, the location of Birkdale Park, to the south of the Southport town centre, was similar to that of Hesketh Park in the north. The amenities of Southport were equally convenient for the residents of both suburbs, but those of Birkdale Park could enjoy them whilst paying the marginally lower Birkdale rate. Even Birkdale Urban District Council's own Year Book was to describe Birkdale as "a popular suburb of Southport."[5]

Birkdale Local Board, and later the Urban District Council, were unfailingly zealous in maintaining tight control of their spending and thus keeping the rates down. Loans were eschewed and expense was largely confined to such necessary items as roads and sewers. This approach was supported by the wealthy ratepayers of Birkdale Park. It was residents living inland of the railway who were the principal sufferers from the parsimony of the local authority. Inadequacies in sewers and roads bore most heavily on them. Despite the "windfall" gain of Victoria Park to the west, there was a shortage of coveniently sited recreational facilities east of the railway. Birkdale's long-running public library saga demonstrated the negative attitude of both Birkdale

Park residents and the local authority to "marginal" municipal spending. A library for Birkdale had to wait until the township received a grant of £5,000 from Carnegie in 1905. In contrast, Southport had a central library from 1878, and provided a branch library in its northern suburb of Churchtown as early as 1893. It was only in the closing years of Birkdale's existence as an independent authority that civic pride was actively promoted through such devices as parading the Fire Brigade with its new steam powered engine; developing the attractive Jubilee Avenue in Victoria Park; producing illustrated municipal year books; and extensively using the township's newly adopted coat of arms. The higher public profile of the Council during this period was in marked contrast to the anonymous nature of the authority's existence in its earlier years. Nevertheless, the authority provided the Birkdale Park residents with what they wanted. Its policies helped to preserve the area's social seclusion in the face of what the residents perceived as the threat to their "quietude", which was posed by the large numbers of visitors attracted to neighbouring Southport.

There was certainly a "laissez-faire" attitude in Birkdale – "He who governs least governs best". The wealthy ratepayers were happy in their "Castles in the Sand", with their personal libraries, large grounds, and a neighbourhood in which the mutual gardening endeavours of the residents had created a "garden suburb". A short carriage drive out of the sheltered environment of Birkdale Park gave them access to the wealth of facilities available in Southport. Perhaps the lack of municipal activity in Birkdale and the apparent indifference to civic pride goes some way to explaining the curious failure of Birkdale residents to make much in the way of a philanthropic contribution within the township, whilst contributing generously in other towns.

It was a combination of a lack of financial support for Birkdale's voluntary church schools and crass administrative blundering that led to the imposition, by Central Government, of an unwanted School Board in Birkdale. Philanthropy, which had resulted in Southport having more churches and chapels than public houses, had also ensured that Southport had far more school places than were required. Government inspectors judged that some of these well-supported voluntary schools were amongst the best elementary schools in the north of England. Ironically it was because the 1870 Education Act decreed that Birkdale was an independent School District and could no longer rely on Birkdale children attending nearby schools across the boundary in Southport that the Birkdale crisis was triggered.

The one issue that galvanised the Birkdale authority and the ratepayers into action was the recurring threat of amalgamation with Southport. The geographical case for Birkdale being a suburb of Southport was unanswerable. It was the accident of the location of the boundary between the townships of Southport and Birkdale, on what had previously been very sparsely populated rabbit warrens, which decreed that Birkdale should become an separate authority. That it should seek to maintain this independence was consistent with the interests of Birkdale's most potent political force – the ratepayers of Birkdale Park. The tide of opinion supporting amalgamation turned swiftly, only when it became evident that the price of continuing independence would be much higher Birkdale rates than those obtaining in neighbouring Southport.

How significant was the role of the landowner – Thomas and later Charles Weld-Blundell – in the story of New Birkdale? On inheriting the Estate, Thomas was quick to identify the development strategy which he pursued in Birkdale. The original Kemp plan suggests that he had not identified the potential influence that the presence of Southport would have on development in Birkdale. Nevertheless, he showed that he was a flexible pragmatist, recognising market forces and reacting to them. His scheme to open up development alongside the Southport boundary, featuring a railway station, was clear evidence of his willingness to sacrifice the "plan". Although he was not willing to invest in order to help to create Birkdale Park, he did attempt to ensure its integrity as a high-class residential suburb by the use of restrictive covenants. It was, however, during the early years of sluggish growth that he allowed mixed development to take place in Birkdale Park, particularly in Aughton Road, in order to raise much needed finance. As it became evident that the Birkdale Park concept was succeeding he became more resolute in maintaining the quality of development. His sale of land to the Birkdale Park Land Company demonstrated his astute business instinct. The control he exercised over the cheaper development which he allowed inland of the railway showed that he, or perhaps his agent, was sensitive to patterns of urban development and the importance of social distance, if house values were to be maintained.

When Charles inherited the estates, his opportunity to further develop Birkdale Park was severely constrained by his father's earlier sale of land to the Birkdale Park Land Company. The challenge this posed allowed him to demonstrate his creativity. His schemes to continue the development of middle-class residential areas, which his father had inaugurated inland of the railway, were imaginative and vigorously pursued. Although he was unsuccessful in his attempt to secure the support of the Local Board for his offer of land for a park inland of the railway, he was able to encourage development along the Liverpool Road axis. He shrewdly used the leasing of land for golf courses as an incentive for suburban development. Perhaps his most imaginative and audacious scheme was the attempt to bulldoze through bungalow development on the foreshore before Birkdale amalgamated with Southport. His handling of the rights' issue on the foreshore demonstrated his resolution and his willingness to use the legal process, backed by his wealth, to frighten off timid opponents such as the Birkdale Council.

Although middle-class development was the priority, he also continued his father's policy of allowing cheaper houses to be built, whilst exercising care to ensure that their location did not constitute a "threat" to more expensive properties. It is interesting to compare the building of the cheapest houses, on and around the old Birkdale Common, with similar development in the detached agricultural village of Crossens to the north of Southport. Birkdale's social blackspot was undoubtedly the Chatham Road area, with its nadir probably in the 1880's. But this area, in which the overspill resettlement of displaced Southport families was occurring, did not compare with the wretched conditions to be found in many of Lancashire's towns and cities. Indeed few could offer the front and back gardens, which were a feature of all the properties in Birkdale.

Administrative independence for Birkdale contradicted the geographical imperatives. New Birkdale was always Southport's suburb; indeed the fall of the land, and thus the natural flow for sewage, was to the north. It was ironic that the problem of providing an efficient sewerage system, which had dogged New Birkdale from its inception, should play a critical role in securing the amalgamation of Southport and Birkdale. The landowner, the local authority, and the residents all had a vested interest in independence, but finally the geographical factors ensured the emergence of a greater Southport which included its suburb Birkdale. Nevertheless, the years of independence have left "Birkdalians" with a strong pride in their heritage. The purpose of this book is to help them and others to understand it.

REFERENCES

ABBREVIATIONS

P.R.O.   Public Record Office, London
M.R.O.   Merseyside Record Office, Liverpool
L.R.O.   Lancashire Record Office, Preston
S.R.L.   Southport Reference Library
B.P.P.   British Parliamentary Papers
B.L.B.   Birkdale Local Board
B.U.D.C.   Birkdale Urban District Council
S.N.D.   Sisters of Notre Dame
T.H.S.L.C. *Transactions of the Historic Society of Lancashire and Cheshire*

CHAPTER ONE

1. M.R.O. 920/WBL/5/8(b) *Solicitor's Accounts 1842–1867.*
2. Liddle, J., "Estate management and land reform politics: The Hesketh and Scarisbrick families and the making of Southport" in Cannandine, D. (ed.), *Patricians, Power and Politics in Nineteenth Century Towns* (1982).
3. *Southport Visiter*, 20 June 1865.
4. See Foster, H.J. *The Influence of Socio-Economic, Spatial and Demographic Factors on the Development of Schooling in a Nineteenth Century Lancashire Residential Town,* M.Ed. thesis, Liverpool University (1976).

CHAPTER TWO

1. *Southport Visiter*, 6 January 1887.
2. *Ibid.*
3. *Southport Visiter*, 6 August 1908.
4. Mutch, A., *Rural Life in South-West Lancashire 1840–1914* (1988), p. 22.
5. *Southport Visiter,* 7 December 1863.
6. *Southport Visiter,* 28 July 1871.
7. *Southport Visiter,* 8 November 1892.
8. *Southport Visiter,* 7 November 1876.
9. *Southport Visiter,* 2 February 1882.
10. *Southport Visiter,* 21 November 1903.
11. *Southport Visiter,* 27 March 1902.
12. *Southport Visiter,* 11 June 1903.
13. S.R.L., *B.U.D.C. General Purposes Committee* 29/5/1903.

14. S.R.L., *B.U.D.C. General Purposes Committee* 30/3/1903.
15. M.R.O. 920/WBL/8/5 *Letter from J.E. Jarratt to C.J. Weld-Blundell* 27/4/1903.
16. S.R.L., *B.U.D.C. Letter to Local Government Board* 5/1/1905.

CHAPTER THREE

1. M.R.O. 920/WBL/5/8(b) *Solicitor's Accounts* 27/11/1848.
2. *Ibid.*, 27/9/1849.
3. *Southport Visiter*, 2 November 1849.
4. L.R.O. DD1n *Draft Lease T. Weld-Blundell & John Jones* 2/2/1849.
5. M.R.O. 920/WBL/5/8(b) *Solicitor's Accounts* 27/8/1853.
6. *Southport Visiter*, 5 December 1984.
7. M.R.O. 920/WBL/1/6 *Weld Blundell Family History* (mss).
8. M.R.O. 920/WBL/5/8(b) *Solicitor's Accounts* 14/4/1851.
9. *Southport Visiter*, 7 February 1854.
10. *St. James' Birkdale 1857–1957* (1957), p. 9.
11. M.R.O. 920/WBL/4/15 *John Rimmer's Lease* 24/6/1851.
12. M.R.O. 920/WBL/5/8(b) *Solicitor's Accounts* 17/10/1851.
13. *Ibid.*, 13/12/1854.
14. Banks, J.A., *Prosperity and Parenthood: A Study of Family Planning among the Victorian Middle Classes* (1954), p. 84.
15. Anderson, G., "The service occupations of nineteenth-century Liverpool" in Anderson, B.L. & Stoney, P.J.M. (eds.), *Commerce, Industry and Transport: Studies in Economic Change in Merseyside* (1983), p. 91.
16. *Southport Visiter*, 10 January 1863.
17. M.R.O. 920/WBL/5/8(b) *Solicitor's Accounts* 11/10/1852.
18. *Southport Visiter*, 24 March 1866.
19. *Southport Visiter*, 27 July 1853.
20. *Southport Visiter*, 16 February 1882.
21. Anon., *Progress of Birkdale as a Health Resort* (1882), p. 8
22. S.R.L. *B.L.B. Highway Committee* 18/5/1870.
23. M.R.O. 920/WBL/5/8(b) *Solicitor's Accounts* 16/11/1867.
24. B.P.P. *Report of the Royal Commission on Secondary Education* 1894–1895, vol. VI., p. 235.
25. Most of the material on private schools is drawn from: Foster, H.J., *Variations in the Provision of Secondary Education in the Nineteenth Century: A Regional Study*, PhD thesis, University of Liverpool (1988).
26. Wood, E.A., *Memorials of James Wood LLD, J.P.* (1902), p. 2.
27. B.P.P., *Report of the Schools Inquiry Commission* (1868), vol. IX., p. 535.
28. Quoted in Marsden, W.E., *Unequal Educational Provision in England and Wales: The Nineteenth-Century Roots* (1987), p. 238.
29. *Southport Visiter*, 6 August 1857.
30. Taylor, H., *Notes on the History of St. James' Church* (mss. 1910), preface.
31. *St. James' Birkdale 1857–1957* (1957), p. 8.
32. *Ibid.*, p.13.

CHAPTER FOUR

1. *Southport Visiter*, 17 July 1887.
2. *Southport Visiter*, 3 August 1875.
3. *Southport Visiter*, 10 January 1871.
4. *Southport Visiter*, 15 February 1876.
5. *Southport Visiter*, 23 May 1876.
6. *Southport Visiter*, 20 December 1883.
7. *Southport Visiter*, 10 July 1882.
8. *Southport Visiter*, 18 May 1882.
9. *Southport Visiter*, 6 July 1882.
10. *Southport Visiter*, 2 September 1884.
11. *Ibid.*
12. *Southport Visiter*, 21 August 1900.
13. *Southport Visiter*, 3 March 1903.
14. *Southport Visiter*, 29 May 1897.
15. *Southport Visiter*, 18 May 1897.
16. *Southport Visiter*, 23 June 1900.
17. *Southport Visiter*, 25 January 1908.
18. Quoted in *Southport Visiter*, 16 October 1888.
19. *Southport Visiter*, 4 February 1909.
20. *Southport Visiter*, 28 July 1888.
21. *Southport Visiter*, 7 August 1906.
22. *Southport Visiter*, 11 November 1897.
23. *Southport Visiter*, 6 May 1879.
24. Quoted in *Southport Visiter*, 6 December 1888.
25. *Southport Visiter*, 9 May 1907.
26. *Southport Visiter*, 26 July 1887.
27. *Southport Visiter*, 24 February 1900.
28. Alexander, A., *Southport Physical Training College* (1901).
29. Guggenheim, O., "Memories of Terra Nova 1912–1917" in *Terra Nova 75th Anniversary Brochure* (1972).
30. Walker, P.N., *The Liverpool Competition: A study of the development of Cricket on Merseyside* (1988), p. 43. For further details of the Birkdale Club see an unpublished history: Porter, K.H., *Twelve Decades of Cricket 1859–1979; Being the Story of Southport and Birkdale Cricket Club* (1979).
31. Johnson, A.J.D., *The History of The Royal Birkdale Golf Club 1889–1989* (1989), p. 11.
32. *Southport Visiter*, 17 April 1894.
33. *Southport Visiter*, 2 June 1898.

CHAPTER FIVE

1. S.R.L. *B.L.B. Highway Committee* 1/10/1869.
2. *Southport Visiter*, 27 February 1904.
3. *Southport Guardian*, 14 April 1888.

4. S.R.L. *B.L.B. Highway and Sewage Committee* 4/6/1878.
5. *Southport Guardian*, 3 December 1889.
6. Jervis, R. *Lancashire Crime and Criminals* (1908), p. 50.
7. *Southport Visiter*, 4 February 1897.
8. S.R.L. *B.L.B. Highway and Sewage Committee* 1879.
9. *Southport Visiter*, 19 June 1909.
10. S.N.D., *The History of the Sisters of Notre Dame in Birkdale 1868–1968* (1968).
11. Moore, J., *The Church of St. Peter Birkdale 1872–1972* (1972), p. 2.
12. S.R.L. *B.L.B. Highway and Sewage Committee* 27/9/1880.
13. *Southport Visiter*, 29 April 1883.
14. *Southport Visiter*, 29 December 1896.
15. For details of elementary schooling in Birkdale see: Foster, H.J. *op.cit.*, (1976).
16. *Southport Visiter*, 23 August 1883.
17. *Southport Guardian*, 12 October 1891.
18. *Southport Visiter*, 15 July 1886.
19. *Birkdale Board School Log Book* 29/3/1888.
20. *Birkdale Board School Log Book* 6/10/1886.
21. *Southport Visiter*, 13 August 1908.
22. Johnson, A.J.D., *The History of the Royal Birkdale Golf Club 1889–1989* (1989), p. 22.
23. Foster, F., "Why don't they play the sort of games we used to?" in *Southport Visiter*, 22 October to 12 November 1993.
24. *Southport Visiter*, 17 July 1888.
25. *Southport Visiter*, 7 February 1905.
26. *Southport Visiter*, 10 August 1905.
27. *Ibid.*
28. Taylor, A.J.P., *A Personal History* (1983), pp. 1–17.

CHAPTER SIX

1. S.R.L. *B.L.B. Board Minutes* 1/9/1889.
2. *Southport Visiter*, 7 October 1889.
3. *Southport Visiter*, 10 August 1901.
4. *Southport Visiter*, 7 November 1905.
5. *Southport Visiter*, 31 June 1891.

CHAPTER SEVEN

1. Miss Swift, "Notes on the History of Birkdale 1850–1874" in Taylor, H., *Notes on the History of St. James' Church* (mss.1910), p. 6.
2. P.R.O. Ed.16/188. *L.E.A. Supply File – Birkdale*.
3. Mutch, A., *Rural Life in South-West Lancashire 1840–1914* (1988), p. 9.
4. Weld-Blundell, C.J., *What's Wrong with England* (1919), p. 72.
5. M.R.O. 920/WBL/5/8(b) *Solicitor's Accounts* 13/3/1852.

6. S.R.L., *B.U.D.C. Health and Cemetery Committee* 25/8/1893.
7. Miss Swift, *op.cit.*, p.5.
8. *St. James' C.E. School Log Book* 1862–1878.
9. Glazebrook, T.K. *A Guide to South-port, North Meoles, in the County of Lancaster: with a brief account of the places in its immediate neighbourhood* (1809), pp. 75–77.
10. M.R.O. 920/WBL/5/8(b) *Solicitor's Accounts* 1/7/1854.
11. *Southport Visiter*, 30 July 1855.
12. *Southport Visiter*, 8 January 1889.
13. *Southport Visiter*, 4 June 1889.
14. Weld-Blundell, C.J., *op.cit.*, p. 186.
15. *Southport Visiter* 25 November 1886.
16. M.R.O. 920/WBL/5/13.
17. S.R.L., *B.U.D.C. Health, Cemetery and Plans Committee* 24/4/1897.
18. *Southport Visiter*, 7 June 1872.
19. *Southport Visiter*, 3 September 1872.
20. S.R.L., *B.L.B. Highway Committee* 23/7/1874.
21. *Southport Visiter*, 10 & 29 October 1910.
22. See Foster. H.J. *op.cit.* (1976), for further details of this school.
23. *Southport Visiter*, 20 May 1848.
24. *Southport Visiter*, 19 August 1859.
25. B.P.P. *Report of the Schools' Inquiry Commission* (1868), vol. IX., p. 703.
26. *Southport Methodist Magazine* vol.XVI. No.3., March 1935.
27. *Southport Visiter*, 8 July 1882.
28. *Southport Visiter*, 25 January 1888.
29. *Southport Visiter*, 8 May 1906.
30. See: Foster, H.J., *Links along the Line: The Story of the Development of Golf in South-West Lancashire* (forthcoming).
31. S.R.L., *B.U.D.C. Health and Cemetery Committee* 26/3/1895.
32. S.R.L., *B.U.D.C. Health and Cemetery Committee* 7/3/1874.
33. Weld-Blundell, C.J., *op.cit.*, p. 164.

CHAPTER EIGHT

1. M.R.O. 920/WBL/5/8(b) *Solicitor's Accounts* January to May 1856.
2. L.R.O. DD In 55/189 *Weld-Blundell papers*.
3. M.R.O. 920/WBL/5/8(b) *Solicitor's Accounts* May to June 1855.
4. S.R.L., *B.U.D.C. Highways and Sewage Committee* 7/7/1893.
5. *Ibid.*, Letter from the Duchy of Lancaster, 9/3/1894.
6. S.R.L. *B.U.D.C. General Purposes Committee* 4/8/1903.
7. M.R.O. 920/WBL/5/12 *Licensed Fishermen*.
8. M.R.O. 920/WBL/8/2 *Engineer's Report*.
9. M.R.O. 920/WBL/5/kk *Correspondence – Septier Fils (Shellfish Seller) Arachon, France*.
10. Weld-Blundell, C.J., *What's Wrong with England* (1919).

CHAPTER NINE

1. Beardwood, F., *Notes on the History of Formby* (1970), p. 30.
2. Kelly, E., *The Viking Village: The Story of Formby* (1973), pp. 73–77.
3. See: Hull, R.C., *Social Differentiation in a North Liverpool Suburb: The case of Great Crosby and Waterloo*, M.A. thesis University of Liverpool (1989).
4. "Southport Inside Out", pt. I, *Bootle Times*, 13 March 1888.
5. B.U.D.C. *Borough Guide to Birkdale* (1910).

SOURCES

Archives
Southport Reference Library
North Meols Vestry   Minutes & rate books
Birkdale Local Board   Minutes & rate books
Birkdale Urban District Council Minutes
Ainsdale Parish Council   Minutes
Census Enumerators' Returns 1851, 1861, 1871, 1881, 1891.

Merseyside Record Office
920 WB Weld-Blundell of Ince Blundell Muniments

Lancashire Record Office
DDIn Blundell of Ince Blundell Muniments

Public Record Office, London
Ed 7/67   Preliminary Statements
Ed 15/20   Private School File
Ed 16/188 Local Education Authority Supply File
Ed 21/100 Public Elementary School Files

Birkdale Schools
Farnborough Road County Primary:
St. James' & St. John's   – Log Books and Registers
Birkdale County Primary:
Birkdale Board School   – Log Books and Registers
St. Teresa's R.C. Inf:
St. Joseph's & St. Teresa's – Log Books and Registers

The Mark Chatterton Collection
Southport & Cheshire Lines Extension Railway Company – Prospectus, share certificates, annual reports & correspondence

Books
Anderson, B.L. & Stoney, P .(eds.), *Commerce, Industry and Transport: Studies in Economic Change on Merseyside*, Liverpool University Press (1983).
Anon., *Birkdale near Southport. An Account of its development as a Health Resort*, Bell, Lancaster (1882).

Ashton, W.M., *The Evolution of a Coastline*, Southport (1920).

B.U.D.C., *Borough Guide to Birkdale*, Southport (1910).

Bailey, F.A., *History of Southport*, Southport (1955).

Banks, J.A., *Prosperity and Parenthood: A Study of Family Planning among the Victorian Middle Classes*, Routledge and Kegan Paul (1954).

Beardwood, F., *Notes on the History of Formby*, Formby (1970).

Bland, E., *Annals of Southport and District*, Southport (1903).

Bland, E., *A Souvenir of Southport Methodism 1811–1911*, Southport (1911).

Bulpit, W.T., *Notes on Southport and District*, Southport (1903).

Butterworth, E., *A Statistical Sketch of the County Palatine of Lancashire*, 1841 reprinted LCAS (1968).

Cannadine, D., (ed.) *Patricians, Power and Politics in Nineteenth Century Towns*, Leicester University Press (1982).

Farrer, W., *A History of the Parish of North Meols*, Liverpool (1903).

Fleetwood-Hesketh, P., *Lancashire Architectural Guide*, John Murray (1955).

Foster, J., *Pedigrees of the County Families of England*, Vol. I. Lancashire (1873).

Glazebrook, T.K., *A Guide to South-port, North Meoles, in the County of Lancaster*, Warrington (1809).

Greenwood, C., *Thatch, Towers and Colonnades: The History of Architecture in Southport*, Southport (1971).

Harrop, S., *Old Birkdale and Ainsdale: Life on the south-west Lancashire Coast 1600-1851*, Southport (1985).

Harrop, S., (ed.) *Families and Cottages of Old Birkdale and Ainsdale*, Carnegie (1992).

Jacson, C., *Formby Reminiscences* Wells, Gardener, Darten & Co. (1897).

Jarratt, E.J., *Municipal Recollections: Southport 1900–1930*, Southport (1931),

Jervis, R., *Lancashire Crime and Criminals*, Southport (1908).

Johnson, A.J.D., *The History of the Royal Birkdale Golf Club*, Southport (1988).

Johnson & Green, *A Guide to Southport*, Southport (1868).

Kelly, E., (ed.) *Viking Village. The Story of Formby*, Formby Society (1973).

Mannex, P. & Co., *History, Topography and Directory of Mid-Lancashire*, Preston (1866).

Marsden, W.E., *Unequal Educational Provision in England and Wales: The Nineteenth-Century Roots*, Woburn Press (1987).

Mutch, A., *Rural Life in South-West Lancashire*, Centre for N.W. Regional Studies (1988).

Nightingale, B., *Lancashire Nonconformity*, Vol. VI. J. Heywood, Manchester (1893).

Pevsner, N., *The Buildings of England: North Lancashire*, Penguin (1969).

Pike, W.J., (ed.) *Contemporary Biographies*, Pike, Brighton (1903).

Searby, P., (ed.) *Educating the Victorian Middle Classes*, History of Education Society (1982).

Sumner, J.R., *A Guide to Southport and the surrounding Neighbourhood and Parish*, Liverpool (1849).

Taylor, A.J.P., *A Personal History*, London (1983).

Walker, P.N., *The Liverpool Competition: A Study of the Development of Cricket on Merseyside*, Countrywise (1988).

Watson, R.C. & McClintock, M.E., *Traditional Houses of the Fylde*, Centre for N.W. Regional Studies (1979).

Weld-Blundell, C.J., *What's Wrong with England?*, Weld-Blundell, London (1919).

Wood, E.A., *Memorial of James Wood L.LD., J.P.*, Charles Kelly (1902).

Theses, Articles, Pamphlets etc.

Anon., "Liverpool Road Church", *Southport Methodist Magazine*, March 1935.

Alexander, A., *Southport Physical Training College* (1901).

Barnes, G.H., *Birkdale Park and North End of the Border of "The Common"*, Birkdale Civic Society (1984).

Barnes, G.H., *"Birkdale Common" and South End to the Border of Ainsdale*, Birkdale Civic Society (1985).

Batham, A., *Leighton College Prospectus*, c. 1900.

Bray, D., *A Glimpse of Life in Birkdale in the 1890s*, mss. undated.

Foster, H.J., *The Influence of Socio-Economic, Spatial and Demographic Factors on the Development of Schooling in a Nineteenth Century Lancashire Residential Town*, M.Ed. thesis, University of Liverpool (1976).

Foster, H.J., *Variation in the Provision of Secondary Education in the Nineteenth Century: A Regional Study*, Ph.D. thesis, University of Liverpool (1988).

Glasgow, E., *Victorian Birkdale*, mss. undated.

Glasgow, E., *Two Birkdale Residents*, mss. undated.

Guggenheim, O., *Memories of Terra Nova 1912–1917*.

Homan, R. & Rowley, G., "The Location of Institutions during the process of urban growth: a case study of churches and chapels in nineteenth century Sheffield", *East Midland Geographer*, vol. 7, 1978–81.

Hatch, J. & Sons, *"Birkdale Lodge" Sale Catalogue* (1914).

Hull, R., *Social Differentiation in a North Liverpool Suburb: the Case of Great Crosby and Waterloo*, M.A. thesis, University of Liverpool (1989).

Lawton, R., "The population of Liverpool in the mid-Nineteenth Century", *T.H.S.L.C.*, vol. 107, 1955.

Marsden, W.E., *The Development of the Educational Facilities of Southport 1825–1944*, M.A. thesis, University of Sheffield (1959).

Moore, J., *The Church of St. Peter 1872–1972*, Southport (1972).

Perkin, H.J., "The Social Tone of the Victorian Seaside Resorts", *Northern History*, vol. IX, 1975.

Pooley, C.G., "Residential differentiation in Victorian Cities: a Reassessment", *The Institute of British Geographers*, NS vol. 9 No. 4, 1984.

Pope, W.B., *A Memoir of John Fernley, Esq., J.P. late of Clairville*, Southport (1874).

Porter, K.H., *Twelve Decades of Cricket 1859–1979 being the Story of the Southport and Birkdale Cricket Club*, mss. (1980).

Reeder, D,. *Suburbanity and the Victorian City*, University of Leicester (1984).

S.N.D., *The History of the Sisters of Notre Dame in Birkdale 1868–1968*, Southport (1968).

Taylor, H., *Notes on the History of St. James' Church, Birkdale*, mss. (1910).

Wright, G., "The Blundell Arms", *Southport Visiter*, 20 April 1990.

INDEX OF NAMES

INDEX OF SUBJECTS

184

Birkdale: Street Plan

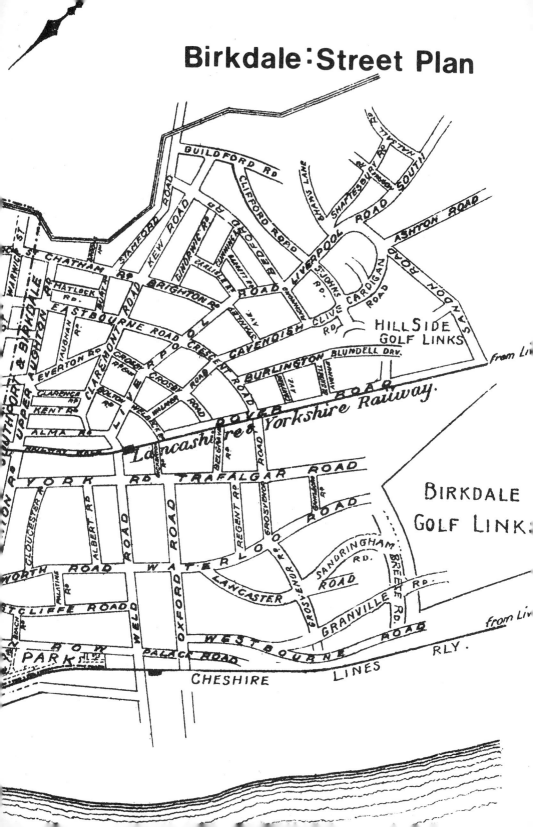